A BALANCED MATHEMATICS PROGRAM INTEGRATING SCIENCE AND LANGUAGE ARTS

Unit Resource Guide
Unit 12
Using Fractions

THIRD EDITION

KENDALL/HUNT PUBLISHING COMPANY
4050 Westmark Drive   Dubuque, Iowa 52002

A TIMS® Curriculum
University of Illinois at Chicago

UIC The University of Illinois
at Chicago

The original edition was based on work supported by the National Science Foundation under grant No. MDR 9050226 and the University of Illinois at Chicago. Any opinions, findings, and conclusions or recommendations expressed in this publication are those of the author(s) and do not necessarily reflect the views of the granting agencies.

Letter Home

Using Fractions

Date: _____

Dear Family Member:

In this unit, your child will use pattern blocks to explore fractions. For example, the figure on the right shows how a student might use pattern blocks to solve the following problem: *Carl ordered a pizza. One-half of the pizza had sausage on it. One-half of that half also had mushrooms. What fraction of the pizza had sausage and mushrooms?* The number sentence $\frac{1}{2} \times \frac{1}{2} = \frac{1}{4}$ represents this problem.

Using pattern block pieces in their investigation of fractions and engaging in other activities such as paper folding, students explore patterns to help them develop paper-and-pencil methods for multiplying fractions.

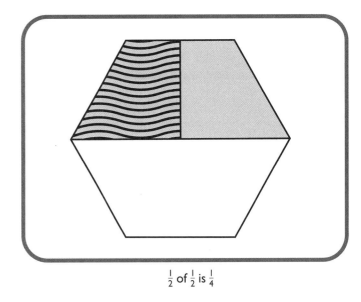

$\frac{1}{2}$ of $\frac{1}{2}$ is $\frac{1}{4}$

During this unit, your child will also explore mixed numbers. Students will find different ways to name mixed numbers. For example, $\frac{13}{4}$ can also be named as $3\frac{1}{4}$ or 2 and $\frac{5}{4}$. They will apply this skill as they add mixed numbers.

As we work through this unit:

- Encourage your child to draw pictures and explain to you the strategies he or she uses to solve homework problems involving fractions.
- Ask your child to share the Adventure Book *Peanut Soup*.
- Help your child review for the midterm test by having him or her share the *Party Problems* with you.

Sincerely,

_____

Carta al hogar

Usando fracciones

Fecha: _____

Estimado miembro de familia:

En esta unidad, su hijo/a usará bloques patrón para explorar fracciones. Por ejemplo, la figura a la derecha muestra de qué manera un estudiante podría usar bloques patrón para resolver el siguiente problema: *Carl encargó una pizza. La mitad de la pizza tenía salchicha. La mitad de esa mitad también tenía champiñones. ¿Qué fracción de la pizza tenía salchicha y champiñones?* La oración numérica $\frac{1}{2} \times \frac{1}{2} = \frac{1}{4}$ representa este problema.

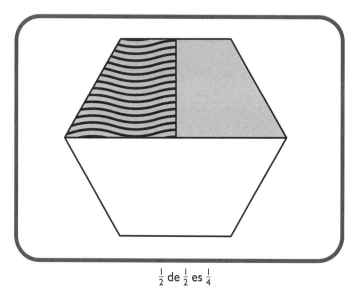

$\frac{1}{2}$ de $\frac{1}{2}$ es $\frac{1}{4}$

Usando los bloques patrón en sus investigaciones de fracciones y realizando otras actividades como doblar papel, los estudiantes explorarán patrones que les ayudarán a desarrollar métodos de papel y lápiz para multiplicar fracciones.

Durante esta unidad, su hijo también explorará los números mixtos. Los estudiantes hallarán diferentes maneras de nombrar los números mixtos. Por ejemplo, $\frac{13}{4}$ también puede tener los siguientes nombres: $3\frac{1}{4}$ ó 2 y $\frac{5}{4}$. Los estudiantes aplicarán esta habilidad al sumar números mixtos.

A medida que avancemos en esta unidad:

- Aliente a su hijo/a a hacer dibujos y explicarle a usted las estrategias que usa para resolver los problemas de la tarea que incluyen fracciones.
- Pídale a su hijo/a que le cuente la historia del Libro de Aventuras titulada *Sopa de cacahuetes*.
- Ayude a su hijo/a a repasar para un examen, pidiéndole que comparta con usted los *Problemas de fiesta*.

Atentamente,

_____

Table of Contents

Unit 12
Using Fractions

Outline
Using Fractions

Estimated Class Sessions

7-9

Unit Summary

Students continue their study of fractions by using pattern blocks and other models to represent fractions in different ways. This helps students generalize concepts and procedures that they can then apply in new situations. For example, they use pattern blocks to model addition of mixed numbers and multiplication of fractions to develop paper-and-pencil methods for these operations. They read an Adventure Book *Peanut Soup,* which uses the context of the work of George Washington Carver to explore the use of fractions in a real-life setting. The unit concludes with a *Midterm Test,* which assesses concepts and skills studied in this and previous units.

Major Concept Focus

- using patterns to build number sense
- multiplying fractions and whole numbers
- multiplying fractions
- estimating the product of fractions
- using fractions in everyday situations
- communicating mathematically
- renaming mixed numbers
- adding mixed numbers
- Student Rubric: *Solving*
- *Adventure Book:* fractions
- midterm test

Pacing Suggestions

This unit is designed to be completed in 7 to 9 days.

- Lesson 6 *Peanut Soup* is an *Adventure Book* story taken from a true incident in the life of George Washington Carver. Students can read this story during language arts or social studies time.

- Lesson 7 *Party Problems* is an optional lesson in which students solve multistep word problems. Assigning these problems for homework can prepare students for the midterm test in Lesson 8. They are also appropriate for a substitute teacher since preparation is minimal.

Assessment Indicators

Use the following Assessment Indicators and the *Observational Assessment Record* that follows the Background section in this unit to assess students on key ideas.

A1. Can students add and subtract fractions using pattern blocks and paper and pencil?

A2. Can students reduce fractions to lowest terms?

A3. Can students rename mixed numbers?

A4. Can students estimate sums of mixed numbers?

A5. Can students add mixed numbers using pattern blocks and paper and pencil?

A6. Can students estimate products of fractions?

A7. Can students multiply a fraction and a whole number?

A8. Can students multiply fractions using pattern blocks, paper folding, and paper and pencil?

A9. Do students solve problems in more than one way?

Unit Planner

KEY: SG = Student Guide, DAB = Discovery Assignment Book, AB = Adventure Book, URG = Unit Resource Guide, DPP = Daily Practice and Problems, HP = Home Practice (found in Discovery Assignment Book), and TIG = Teacher Implementation Guide.

	Lesson Information	Supplies	Copies/ Transparencies
Lesson 1 **Hexagon Duets** URG Pages 20–29 SG Pages 376–379 DAB Page 193 DPP A–B *Estimated Class Sessions* **1-2**	**Activity** Addition of mixed numbers is introduced through the use of a game. Students find equivalent representations of mixed numbers. **Math Facts** DPP Bit A reviews the last six division facts. **Homework** Assign the Homework section in the *Student Guide.* **Assessment** 1. Use the Journal Prompt as an assessment. 2. Use *Question 1* of the Homework section to assess students' abilities to rename mixed numbers. 3. Use the *Observational Assessment Record* to note students' abilities to add mixed numbers.	• 1 set of pattern blocks (2–3 yellow hexagons, 6 red trapezoids, 10 blue rhombuses, 10 green triangles, 6 brown trapezoids, 12 purple triangles) per student pair • 1 spinner or paper clip and pencil per student group • overhead pattern blocks, optional	• 1 transparency of *Hexagon Duets Spinner* DAB Page 193, optional • 1 copy of *Observational Assessment Record* URG Pages 11–12 to be used throughout this unit
Lesson 2 **Adding Mixed Numbers** URG Pages 30–37 SG Pages 380–382 DPP C–D HP Parts 1–2 *Estimated Class Sessions* **1**	**Activity** Students model addition of mixed numbers using pattern blocks; then they develop paper-and-pencil methods. **Homework** 1. Assign the homework problems in the *Student Guide.* 2. Assign Parts 1–2 of the Home Practice. **Assessment** Use *Questions 3–4* of the Homework section as an assessment.	• 1 set of pattern blocks (2–3 yellow hexagons, 6 red trapezoids, 10 blue rhombuses, 10 green triangles, 6 brown trapezoids, 12 purple triangles) per student pair • overhead pattern blocks, optional	
Lesson 3 **Fractions of Groups** URG Pages 38–48 SG Pages 383–386 DPP E–F *Estimated Class Sessions* **1**	**Activity** Using diagrams, students develop procedures for multiplying a fraction times a whole number. **Math Facts** DPP Bit E reviews the last six division facts. **Homework** Assign the Homework section in the *Student Guide.* **Assessment** Use *Question 7* in the Homework section as an assessment.		

	Lesson Information	**Supplies**	**Copies/ Transparencies**
Lesson 4 **Multiplication of Fractions** URG Pages 49–60 SG Pages 387–389 DAB Pages 195–197 DPP G–H *Estimated Class Sessions* 	**Activity** Using pattern blocks, students multiply fractions times whole numbers and fractions times fractions. **Math Facts** DPP Bit G reviews the last six facts. **Homework** Assign the Homework section in the *Student Guide.* **Assessment** 1. Use DPP Task H as a quiz to assess students' abilities to add mixed numbers. 2. Check students' homework for their abilities to represent fractions using pattern blocks and number sentences.	• 1 set of pattern blocks (2–3 yellow hexagons, 6 red trapezoids, 10 blue rhombuses, 10 green triangles, 6 brown trapezoids, 12 purple triangles) per student pair • overhead pattern blocks, optional	• 1 transparency of *Pattern Block Record Sheet* DAB Pages 195–197, optional
Lesson 5 **Using Patterns to Multiply Fractions** URG Pages 61–70 SG Pages 390–391 DPP I–J HP Parts 3–4 *Estimated Class Sessions* 	**Activity** Students fold paper to model multiplication of fractions. The patterns they see help them develop procedures for multiplying fractions with paper and pencil. **Math Facts** DPP Bit I reviews math facts in number sentences with variables. **Homework** 1. Assign the Homework section in the *Student Guide.* 2. Assign Parts 3 and 4 of the Home Practice. 3. Use some or all of the *Party Problems* in Lesson 7 for homework. **Assessment** 1. Use *Questions 10–14* in the Homework section as an assessment. 2. Use the *Observational Assessment Record* to note students' abilities to multiply fractions. 3. Transfer your observations to students' *Individual Assessment Record Sheets.*	• several $8\frac{1}{2}$-by-11 inch sheets of scrap paper per student • crayons or colored pencils	• 1 copy of *Individual Assessment Record Sheet* TIG Assessment section per student, previously copied for use throughout the year
Lesson 6 **Peanut Soup** URG Pages 71–80 AB Pages 77–92 DPP K–L HP Parts 5–6 *Estimated Class Sessions* 	**Adventure Book** The story tells how George Washington Carver was able to convince businessmen of the economic value of peanuts by inviting them to a meal made from peanut products. As they prepare the meal, Carver's students use fractions to convert recipes to the needed size. **Math Facts** DPP Bit K reviews math facts in division sentences with quotients as mixed numbers. **Homework** Assign Parts 5 and 6 of the Home Practice.		

(Continued)

	Lesson Information	Supplies	Copies/Transparencies
Lesson 7 **Party Problems** URG Pages 81–85 SG Pages 392–393 *Estimated Class Sessions* **1**	OPTIONAL LESSON **Optional Activity** Students solve word problems in the context of a birthday party. **Homework** Assign some or all of the problems for homework.	• 1 calculator per student	
Lesson 8 **Midterm Test** URG Pages 86–100 DPP M–N HP Part 7 *Estimated Class Sessions* **1**	**Assessment Activity** Students complete a test involving concepts covered in this and previous units. **Math Facts** DPP Bit M reviews the last six facts. **Homework** 1. Assign DPP Task N for homework. 2. Assign Part 7 of the Home Practice. **Assessment** Add this test to students' portfolios to compare to similar assessments.	• pattern blocks • 1 ruler per student • 1 calculator per student	• 1 copy of *Midterm Test* URG Pages 91–96 per student

Preparing for Upcoming Lessons

Begin collecting lids and cans of different sizes for the lab *Circumference vs. Diameter* in Unit 14.

Connections

A current list of literature and software connections is available at *www.mathtrailblazers.com.* You can also find information on connections in the *Teacher Implementation Guide* Literature List and Software List sections.

Literature Connections

Suggested Titles

- Adair, Gene. *George Washington Carver: Botanist.* Chelsea House Publishers, New York, 1989. (Lesson 6)
- Carter, Andy, and Carol Saller. *George Washington Carver.* Carolrhoda Books, Inc., Minneapolis, MN, 2001. (Lesson 6)
- Mitchell, Barbara. *A Pocketful of Goobers.* Carolrhoda Books, Inc., Minneapolis, MN, 1989. (Lesson 6)
- Moore, Eva. *The Story of George Washington Carver.* Scholastic, New York, 1995. (Lesson 6)

Software Connections

- *Fraction Attraction* develops understanding of fractions using fraction bars, pie charts, hundreds blocks, and other materials.
- *Math Arena* is a collection of math activities that reinforces many math concepts.
- *Math Munchers Deluxe* provides practice with basic facts and finding equivalent fractions, decimals, percents, ratios, angles and identifying geometric shapes, factors, and multiples in an arcade-like game.
- *Math Mysteries: Advanced Fractions* develops multistep problem solving with fractions.
- *Mighty Math Number Heroes* poses short answer questions about different math topics including fractions.
- *National Library of Virtual Manipulatives* website (http://matti.usu.edu) allows students to work with manipulatives including pattern blocks.
- *Tenth Planet: Fraction Operations* develops conceptual understanding of fraction operations, including finding common denominators.

Teaching All Math Trailblazers Students

Math Trailblazers® lessons are designed for students with a wide range of abilities. The lessons are flexible and do not require significant adaptation for diverse learning styles or academic levels. However, when needed, lessons can be tailored to allow students to engage their abilities to the greatest extent possible while building knowledge and skills.

To assist you in meeting the needs of all students in your classroom, this section contains information about some of the features in the curriculum that allow all students access to mathematics. For additional information, see the Teaching the *Math Trailblazers* Student: Meeting Individual Needs section in the *Teacher Implementation Guide.*

Differentiation Opportunities in this Unit

Games

Use games to promote or extend understanding of math concepts and to practice skills with children who need more practice.

- Lesson 1 *Hexagon Duets*

Journal Prompts

Journal prompts provide opportunities for students to explain and reflect on mathematical problems. They can help both students who need practice explaining their ideas and students who benefit from answering higher order questions. Students with various learning styles can express themselves using pictures, words, and sentences. Teachers can alter journal prompts to suit students' ability levels. The following lessons contain a journal prompt:

- Lesson 1 *Hexagon Duets*
- Lesson 3 *Fractions of Groups*
- Lesson 5 *Using Patterns to Multiply Fractions*

DPP Challenges

DPP Challenges are items from the Daily Practice and Problems that usually take more than fifteen minutes to complete. These problems are more thought-provoking and can be used to stretch students' problem-solving skills. The following lessons have a DPP Challenge in them:

- DPP Challenge B from Lesson 1 *Hexagon Duets*
- DPP Challenge D from Lesson 2 *Adding Mixed Numbers*

Extensions

Use extensions to enrich lessons. Many extensions provide opportunities to further involve or challenge students of all abilities. Take a moment to review the extensions prior to beginning this unit. Some extensions may require additional preparation and planning. The following lessons contain extensions:

- Lesson 2 *Adding Mixed Numbers*
- Lesson 6 *Peanut Soup*

Background
Using Fractions

In this unit, students continue their study of fractions. The activities build upon and extend previous activities in Units 3, 5, 9, and 11 of fifth grade. All the fraction work in the curriculum is built on a solid conceptual foundation so students can develop and apply procedures and skills. Among the concepts and skills students must acquire is the ability to represent and identify fractions in equivalent forms. The Number and Operations Standard of the *Principles and Standards for School Mathematics* states:

> "Representing numbers with various physical materials should be a major part of mathematics instruction in the elementary school grades. By the middle grades, students should understand that numbers can be represented in various ways, so that they see that $\frac{1}{4}$, 25%, and 0.25 are all different names for the same number. Students' understanding and ability to reason will grow as they represent fractions and decimals with physical materials and on number lines and as they learn to generate equivalent representations of fractions and decimals." (NCTM, 2000)

This unit's activities use pattern blocks to represent various equivalent forms of the same number. Students have many opportunities to move between concrete models and symbolic representations of a number. This ability to read, use, and appreciate multiple representations of the same quantity is a critical step in learning to understand and do mathematics. For example, to add mixed numbers it is important for students to understand that $2\frac{3}{4}$, $2\frac{6}{8}$, and $1\frac{14}{8}$ all represent the same quantity.

Modeling the same fraction in different ways helps students generalize concepts and procedures and apply them to new situations. Using diagrams of collections of objects, paper folding, and pattern blocks, students model multiplication of fractions. They look for patterns to help them find efficient methods for multiplying a whole number times a fraction and a fraction times a fraction. See Figure 1.

As students learn to add mixed numbers and multiply fractions, the focus of instruction is on building conceptual understanding in contrast to teaching rote procedures. This understanding provides a foundation for later work with rational expressions in algebra.

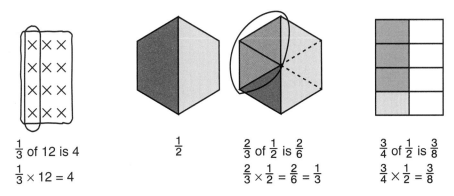

$\frac{1}{3}$ of 12 is 4

$\frac{1}{3} \times 12 = 4$

$\frac{1}{2}$

$\frac{2}{3}$ of $\frac{1}{2}$ is $\frac{2}{6}$

$\frac{2}{3} \times \frac{1}{2} = \frac{2}{6} = \frac{1}{3}$

$\frac{3}{4}$ of $\frac{1}{2}$ is $\frac{3}{8}$

$\frac{3}{4} \times \frac{1}{2} = \frac{3}{8}$

Figure 1: *Three models for multiplying fractions*

Resources

- Behr, M.J., and T.R. Post. "Teaching Rational Number and Decimal Concepts." In *Teaching Mathematics in Grades K–8: Research Based Methods.* Allyn and Bacon, Boston, 1992.

- Burns, Marilyn. *About Teaching Mathematics. A K–8 Resource.* Math Solutions Publications, White Plains, NY, 1992.

- Cramer, K., M. Behr, and T. Post. *Rational Number Project: Lessons for the Middle Grades—Levels 1 and 2.* Kendall/Hunt, Dubuque, IA, 1998.

- Cramer, K., T. Post, and R. del Mas. "Initial Fraction Learning by Fourth- and Fifth-Grade Students: A Comparison of the Effects of Using Commercial Curricula with the Effects of Using the Rational Number Project Curriculum." *Journal for Research in Mathematics Education,* 33(2), pp. 111–144, March 2002.

- Phillips, Elizabeth, et al. *Understanding Rational Numbers and Proportions* from the Curriculum and Evaluation Standards Addenda Series, Grades 5–8. The National Council of Teachers of Mathematics, Reston, VA, 1992.

- *Principles and Standards for School Mathematics.* National Council of Teachers of Mathematics, Reston, VA, 2000.

Observational Assessment Record

(A1) Can students add and subtract fractions using pattern blocks and paper and pencil?

(A2) Can students reduce fractions to lowest terms?

(A3) Can students rename mixed numbers?

(A4) Can students estimate sums of mixed numbers?

(A5) Can students add mixed numbers using pattern blocks and paper and pencil?

(A6) Can students estimate products of fractions?

(A7) Can students multiply a fraction and a whole number?

(A8) Can students multiply fractions using pattern blocks, paper folding, and paper and pencil?

(A9) Do students solve problems in more than one way?

(A10) _____

Name	A1	A2	A3	A4	A5	A6	A7	A8	A9	A10	Comments
1.											
2.											
3.											
4.											
5.											
6.											
7.											
8.											
9.											
10.											
11.											
12.											

Name	A1	A2	A3	A4	A5	A6	A7	A8	A9	A10	Comments
13.											
14.											
15.											
16.											
17.											
18.											
19.											
20.											
21.											
22.											
23.											
24.											
25.											
26.											
27.											
28.											
29.											
30.											
31.											
32.											

Unit 12

Daily Practice and Problems
Using Fractions

A DPP Menu for Unit 12

Two Daily Practice and Problems (DPP) items are included for each class session listed in the Unit Outline. A scope and sequence chart for the DPP is in the *Teacher Implementation Guide*.

Icons in the Teacher Notes column designate the subject matter of each DPP item. The first item in each class session is always a Bit and the second is either a Task or Challenge. Each item falls into one or more of the categories listed below. A menu of the DPP items for Unit 12 follows.

N Number Sense	Computation	Time	Geometry
B, C, F, H–J, L–N	B–D, F, H–N		C, D
Math Facts	$ Money	Measurement	Data
A, E, G, I, K, M	N	B, D	

The *Daily Practice and Problems and Home Practice Guide* in the *Teacher Implementation Guide* includes information on how and when to use the DPP.

Review of Math Facts

By the end of fourth grade, students in *Math Trailblazers* are expected to demonstrate fluency with all the division facts. The DPP for this unit continues the systematic approach to reviewing the division facts. This unit reviews the related division facts in the group of multiplication facts known as the last six facts. Since there are two related division facts for each multiplication fact, there are 12 division facts in this group ($24 \div 6 = 4$, $24 \div 4 = 6$, $28 \div 4 = 7$, $28 \div 7 = 4$, $32 \div 8 = 4$, $32 \div 4 = 8$, $42 \div 6 = 7$, $42 \div 7 = 6$, $48 \div 6 = 8$, $48 \div 8 = 6$, $56 \div 8 = 7$, $56 \div 7 = 8$).

For more information about the distribution and assessment of the math facts, see the TIMS Tutor: *Math Facts* in the *Teacher Implementation Guide* and the *Grade 5 Facts Resource Guide*.

 **Daily Practice and Problems**

Students may solve the items individually, in groups, or as a class. The items may also be assigned for homework. The DPPs are also available on the Teacher Resource CD.

Student Questions	Teacher Notes

A **Practice: Last Six Facts**

A. $48 \div 6 =$ B. $56 \div 8 =$

C. $24 \div 4 =$ D. $32 \div 8 =$

E. $42 \div 6 =$ F. $28 \div 7 =$

TIMS Bit

A. 8   B. 7

C. 6   D. 4

E. 7   F. 4

B **Making a Map**

Frank made a map of his classroom; 1 cm on his map represents 50 centimeters in the classroom. He drew a straight line on his map from the teacher's desk to the garbage can. Then he drew a straight line from the garbage can to the door. He made these measurements:

- The distance from the teacher's desk to the garbage can is 2.4 cm.

- The distance from the garbage can to the door is 4.6 cm.

Use Frank's measurements to predict the actual distance in the classroom from Mr. Moreno's desk to the garbage can, and then to the door.

TIMS Challenge

The predicted total distance is 350 cm or 3.5 m.

Student Questions	Teacher Notes

C Do You See a Triangle?

In each case, tell whether the given lengths will make a triangle. Justify your answer. (*Hint:* Estimation is an appropriate strategy for solving this problem.)

A. 3 inches, 4 inches, 6 inches

B. $3\frac{1}{2}$ inches, 8 inches, $4\frac{5}{8}$ inches

C. $15\frac{3}{16}$ inches, $7\frac{1}{4}$ inches, $7\frac{3}{8}$ inches

Encourage students to estimate for B and C.

A. Yes, because 3 inches + 4 inches > 6 inches

B. Yes, $3\frac{1}{2}$ inches + $4\frac{5}{8}$ inches > 8 inches

C. No, $7\frac{1}{4}$ inches + $7\frac{3}{8}$ inches < 15 inches

---

D Making a Quilt

TIMS Challenge

1. Mrs. Sorenson is teaching the students in Mr. Moreno's class how to make a patchwork quilt. The entire quilt will be a rectangle measuring 4 feet by 5 feet. The quilt will be made up of individual squares, each measuring 6 inches by 6 inches. How many individual squares are needed to make the quilt? Explain how you solved the problem.

2. There are 22 students in Mr. Moreno's class. The students are going to cut the individual squares from scraps of material. How many individual squares should each student cut out to have enough squares for the quilt?

Encourage students to draw a picture to help them solve the problem. Strategies will vary. One possible solution:

1. 4 feet = 48 inches; 5 feet = 60 inches. Eight individual squares can fit along the length of 48 inches. Ten individual squares can fit along the width of 60 inches. 8 × 10 = 80 squares

2. Eight students must cut out 3 squares; 14 students must cut out 4 squares.

Student Questions	Teacher Notes

 E   **Division Facts**

TIMS Bit

A. $240 \div 40 =$

B. $4800 \div 60 =$

C. $2800 \div 700 =$

D. $560 \div 70 =$

E. $42{,}000 \div 600 =$

F. $3200 \div 80 =$

A. 6

B. 80

C. 4

D. 8

E. 70

F. 40

F   **Practicing the Operations**

TIMS Task

Use paper and pencil to solve the following problems. Estimate to be sure your answers are reasonable. For A and B, write your answer (the quotient) as a mixed number. Fractions should be in lowest terms.

1. A. $636 \div 16 =$

    B. $1994 \div 8 =$

    C. $467 \times 8 =$

    D. $37.2 + 125.06 =$

    E. $1045.35 - 76.3 =$

    F. $0.7 \times 85 =$

2. Explain your estimation strategy for 1F.

1. A. $39\frac{12}{16} = 39\frac{3}{4}$

   B. $249\frac{2}{8} = 249\frac{1}{4}$

   C.   3736

   D.   162.26

   E.   969.05

   F.   59.5

2. Seven-tenths (.7) is close to 0.75 or $\frac{3}{4}$. $\frac{3}{4}$ of 80 is 60.

Student Questions	Teacher Notes

G **Division Facts**

Find the number *n* that makes each sentence true.

A. $42 \div 7 = n$ B. $320 \div 4 = n$
C. $56 \div n = 7$ D. $28 \div n = 7$
E. $n \div 6 = 4$ F. $n \div 8 = 6$

TIMS Bit

A. 6   B. 80
C. 8   D. 4
E. 24   F. 48

H **Adding Mixed Numbers**

Use paper and pencil to solve the following problems. Write all fractions in lowest terms. Estimate to see if your answers are reasonable.

A. $8\frac{7}{10} + 2\frac{1}{10} =$
B. $2\frac{5}{9} + 3\frac{1}{3} =$
C. $3\frac{1}{12} + 4\frac{3}{8} =$
D. $5\frac{5}{6} + 2\frac{1}{2} =$
E. $5\frac{7}{10} + 2\frac{3}{5} =$

TIMS Task

A. $10\frac{8}{10} = 10\frac{4}{5}$
B. $5\frac{8}{9}$
C. $7\frac{11}{24}$
D. $8\frac{1}{3}$
E. $8\frac{3}{10}$

I **More Division Fact Practice**

Find the number *n* that makes each sentence true.

A. $56 \div n = 8$
B. $480 \div n = 60$
C. $n \times 400 = 24,000$
D. $80 \times n = 3200$
E. $60 \times n = 420$
F. $n \div 7 = 400$

TIMS Bit

A. 7
B. 8
C. 60
D. 40
E. 7
F. 2800

Student Questions	Teacher Notes

J Granola Bars

Lin's favorite granola bars come in packages of 10.

How many bars are in:

A. $\frac{1}{2}$ of a package?

B. $\frac{1}{10}$ of a package?

C. $\frac{3}{10}$ of a package?

D. $\frac{1}{5}$ of a package?

E. $\frac{3}{5}$ of a package?

F. $1\frac{1}{2}$ packages?

TIMS Task

A. 5

B. 1

C. 3

D. 2

E. 6

F. 15

K Division

Try to solve the following problems in your head. Write the quotients as mixed numbers. Fractions should be in lowest terms.

A. $30 \div 7 =$ B. $60 \div 8 =$

C. $47 \div 6 =$ D. $26 \div 6 =$

E. $51 \div 6 =$ F. $35 \div 4 =$

TIMS Bit

A. $4\frac{2}{7}$ B. $7\frac{1}{2}$

C. $7\frac{5}{6}$ D. $4\frac{1}{3}$

E. $8\frac{1}{2}$ F. $8\frac{3}{4}$

L Multiplying Fractions

Multiply these fractions. Reduce answers to lowest terms. Estimate to see if your answers are reasonable.

A. $\frac{1}{2} \times \frac{1}{4} =$ B. $\frac{1}{4} \times \frac{1}{4} =$

C. $\frac{2}{3} \times \frac{1}{2} =$ D. $\frac{3}{8} \times \frac{1}{6} =$

E. $\frac{5}{8} \times \frac{2}{3} =$ F. $\frac{1}{2} \times \frac{3}{5} =$

TIMS Task

A. $\frac{1}{8}$ B. $\frac{1}{16}$

C. $\frac{2}{6} = \frac{1}{3}$ D. $\frac{3}{48} = \frac{1}{16}$

E. $\frac{10}{24} = \frac{5}{12}$ F. $\frac{3}{10}$

Fact Practice

A. $60 \times 80 =$

B. $420 \div 70 =$

C. $32,000 \div 400 =$

D. $70 \times 8 =$

E. $2400 \div 6 =$

F. $7000 \times 40 =$

TIMS Bit

A. 4800

B. 6

C. 80

D. 560

E. 400

F. 280,000

Inheriting Money

Krista's uncle died and left her his money. In order to claim her fortune, she has to solve this riddle that tells the amount she inherited.

Take your time to find a prime.
But, beware, it's one more than a square.
It's under one hundred and ends in seven.
Now, add six zeros and you'll be in heaven.
Problems, you say, there's more than
one solution?
Then, add them, my dear, and enjoy
your fortune.

How much money did Krista inherit?

TIMS Task

Primes less than 100 and one more than a square:

5, 17, and 37; 17 and 37 end in a 7;
$17,000,000 + $37,000,000 =
$54,000,000

Lesson 1

Hexagon Duets

Estimated Class Sessions

1-2

This lesson has two parts. In the first part, students play a game using pattern blocks to review addition of fractions and to introduce addition of mixed numbers. To help students develop number sense with fractions, this game emphasizes finding sums using manipulatives, rather than procedures.

In the second part of the lesson, students use pattern blocks to explore renaming mixed numbers using equivalent mixed numbers and fractions. They practice these skills, which are prerequisites for adding mixed numbers, using paper-and-pencil methods. The activities in Lesson 2 develop paper-and-pencil methods for adding mixed numbers.

Key Content

- Adding fractions.
- Adding mixed numbers using pattern blocks.
- Renaming mixed numbers.

Math Facts

DPP Bit A reviews the last six division facts.

Homework

Assign the Homework section in the *Student Guide.*

Assessment

1. Use the Journal Prompt as an assessment.
2. Use **Question 1** of the Homework section to assess renaming mixed numbers.
3. Use the *Observational Assessment Record* to note students' abilities to add mixed numbers.

Curriculum Sequence

Before This Unit

In Grade 4 Unit 12 students used pattern blocks to model addition and subtraction of fractions. In Grade 5 Unit 3 Lesson 2, they renamed mixed numbers as improper fractions and improper fractions as mixed numbers using pattern blocks. In Unit 5 Lessons 6 and 7, students used rectangles on dot paper to model addition and subtraction of fractions. In Unit 11 Lesson 6 students added and subtracted fractions using common denominators and reduced fractions to lowest terms.

Materials List

Supplies and Copies

Student	Teacher
Supplies for Each Student Pair • 1 set of pattern blocks (2–3 yellow hexagons, 6 red trapezoids, 10 blue rhombuses, 10 green triangles, 6 brown trapezoids, 12 purple triangles) **Supplies for Each Student Group** • 1 spinner or paper clip and pencil	**Supplies** • overhead pattern blocks, optional
Copies	**Copies/Transparencies** • 1 copy of *Observational Assessment Record* to be used throughout this unit (*Unit Resource Guide* Pages 11–12) • 1 transparency of *Hexagon Duets Spinner,* optional (*Discovery Assignment* Book Page 193)

All blackline masters including assessment, transparency, and DPP masters are also on the Teacher Resource CD.

Student Books
Hexagon Duets (*Student Guide* Pages 376–379)
Hexagon Duets Spinner (*Discovery Assignment Book* Page 193)

Daily Practice and Problems and Home Practice
DPP items A–B (*Unit Resource Guide* Page 14)

Note: Classrooms whose pacing differs significantly from the suggested pacing of the units should use the Math Facts Calendar in Section 4 of the *Facts Resource Guide* to ensure students receive the complete math facts program.

Assessment Tools
Observational Assessment Record (*Unit Resource Guide* Pages 11–12)

Suggestions for using the DPPs are on page 26.

A. Bit: Practice: Last Six Facts (URG p. 14)

A. $48 \div 6 =$ B. $56 \div 8 =$

C. $24 \div 4 =$ D. $32 \div 8 =$

E. $42 \div 6 =$ F. $28 \div 7 =$

B. Challenge: Making a Map
(URG p. 14)

Frank made a map of his classroom; 1 cm on his map represents 50 centimeters in the classroom. He drew a straight line on his map from the teacher's desk to the garbage can. Then he drew a straight line from the garbage can to the door. He made these measurements:

- The distance from the teacher's desk to the garbage can is 2.4 cm.

- The distance from the garbage can to the door is 4.6 cm.

Use Frank's measurements to predict the actual distance in the classroom from Mr. Moreno's desk to the garbage can, and then to the door.

Teaching the Activity

Part 1 Playing *Hexagon Duets*

This game is played in groups of four, with pairs forming teams and playing against another pair. Before play begins, discuss the rules on the *Hexagon Duets* Activity Pages in the *Student Guide*. *Questions 1–3* highlight two important aspects of the game: representing addition problems using pattern blocks and writing number sentences for the resulting sums. To clarify the rules, play a sample round with three students using overhead pattern blocks and a transparency of *Hexagon Duets Spinner* Game Page from the *Discovery Assignment Book*.

As students play, they need not find common denominators to find the sums or reduce their answers to lowest terms. They can simply use the pattern blocks to add and make trades until they can represent the sum as a proper fraction or a mixed number. Instead of concentrating on procedures at this point, encourage students to focus on the reasonableness of the results.

Ask:

- *Should the sums be less than one or more than one? Less than two or more than two?*

TIMS Tip

If clear plastic spinners are not available, students can use an opened paper clip and a pencil as shown in Figure 2. They can also use bobby pins instead of paper clips.

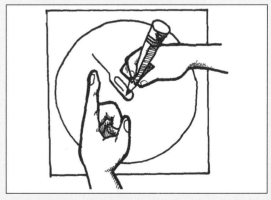

Figure 2: *Using a paper clip as a spinner*

Journal Prompt

While playing a round of *Hexagon Duets*, Alexis spun $\frac{1}{3}$ and $\frac{1}{12}$ and Manny spun $\frac{1}{6}$ and $\frac{1}{4}$. Will their team total be more than one or less than one? How do you know?

Hexagon Duets

Players

This game is played by four players, two players on each team.

Materials

Each group of four players needs:

- pattern blocks
- paper and pencil
- *Hexagon Duets Spinner* Game Page from the *Discovery Assignment Book*, four copies
- a clear, plastic spinner (or a paper clip and a pencil)

Hexagon Duets Spinner

one whole

Rules

1. One yellow hexagon is one whole.
2. Each player takes a turn. On your turn, spin the spinner twice. Each time you spin, place the pattern blocks on the outline of the two hexagons on your *Hexagon Duets Spinner* Game Page. Follow Jackie and Lin's example in Questions 1–3.
3. Add the two fractions together. You may need to trade your pattern blocks for other pattern blocks to find the sum.
4. Write a number sentence for the sum of your two fractions.
5. Add your sum to your partner's sum to find a grand total. Write a number sentence for the grand total.
6. The team with the largest total wins the round and earns $\frac{1}{3}$ of a point.
7. Continue to play more rounds. The first team to earn one whole point is the winner.

376   SG • Grade 5 • Unit 12 • Lesson 1   Hexagon Duets

Student Guide - page 376

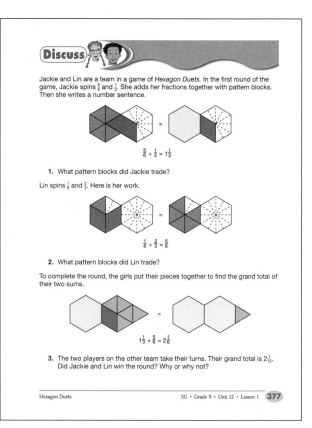

(Discuss)

Jackie and Lin are a team in a game of *Hexagon Duets*. In the first round of the game, Jackie spins $\frac{5}{6}$ and $\frac{1}{2}$. She adds her fractions together with pattern blocks. Then she writes a number sentence.

$$\frac{5}{6} + \frac{1}{2} = 1\frac{1}{3}$$

1. What pattern blocks did Jackie trade?

Lin spins $\frac{1}{6}$ and $\frac{2}{3}$. Here is her work.

$$\frac{1}{6} + \frac{2}{3} = \frac{5}{6}$$

2. What pattern blocks did Lin trade?

To complete the round, the girls put their pieces together to find the grand total of their two sums.

$$1\frac{1}{3} + \frac{5}{6} = 2\frac{1}{6}$$

3. The two players on the other team take their turns. Their grand total is $2\frac{1}{12}$. Did Jackie and Lin win the round? Why or why not?

Hexagon Duets   SG • Grade 5 • Unit 12 • Lesson 1   377

Student Guide - page 377 (Answers on p. 28)

Many Names for Mixed Numbers

When using mixed numbers and fractions, you often need to use different names for the same mixed number. For example, $2\frac{1}{3}$, $2\frac{2}{6}$, and $1\frac{8}{6}$ are all equal.

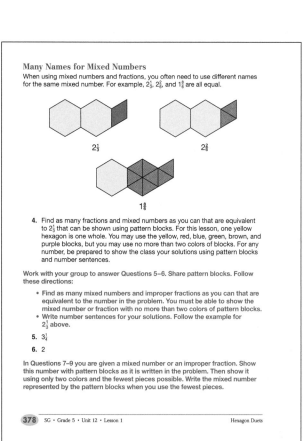

$2\frac{1}{3}$ $2\frac{2}{6}$

$1\frac{8}{6}$

4. Find as many fractions and mixed numbers as you can that are equivalent to $2\frac{1}{3}$ that can be shown using pattern blocks. For this lesson, one yellow hexagon is one whole. You may use the yellow, red, blue, green, brown, and purple blocks, but you may use no more than two colors of blocks. For any number, be prepared to show the class your solutions using pattern blocks and number sentences.

Work with your group to answer Questions 5–6. Share pattern blocks. Follow these directions:

- Find as many mixed numbers and improper fractions as you can that are equivalent to the number in the problem. You must be able to show the mixed number or fraction with no more than two colors of pattern blocks.
- Write number sentences for your solutions. Follow the example for $2\frac{1}{3}$ above.

5. $3\frac{1}{4}$

6. 2

In Questions 7–9 you are given a mixed number or an improper fraction. Show this number with pattern blocks as it is written in the problem. Then show it using only two colors and the fewest pieces possible. Write the mixed number represented by the pattern blocks when you use the fewest pieces.

378   SG • Grade 5 • Unit 12 • Lesson 1   Hexagon Duets

Student Guide - page 378 (Answers on p. 28)

Name _____   Date _____

Hexagon Duets Spinner

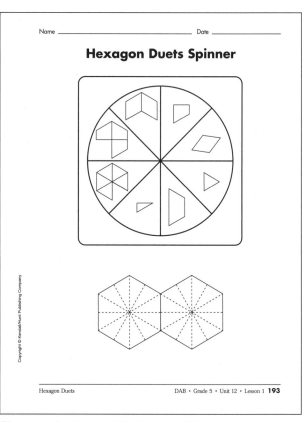

Hexagon Duets   DAB • Grade 5 • Unit 12 • Lesson 1   **193**

Discovery Assignment Book - page 193

Part 2 Many Names for Mixed Numbers

This part of the activity helps students find many equivalent representations of mixed numbers. Understanding equivalence is an important step in many procedures using fractions, including addition of mixed numbers.

Use pattern blocks to represent $2\frac{1}{3}$ as shown in the Many Names for Mixed Numbers section of the *Hexagon Duets* Activity Pages in the *Student Guide*. Ask students to follow your example using their pattern blocks. (They will need to work in groups of three or four to have enough blocks for some of the questions.) Once they show $2\frac{1}{3}$ with blocks, ask them to use the blocks to find as many fractions and mixed numbers as possible that are equivalent to $2\frac{1}{3}$ *(Question 4).* They are to use only one or two block colors in any one mixed number or improper fraction. Encourage students to write a number sentence that shows the equivalence of the various representations. Figure 3 shows five such representations for $2\frac{1}{3}$ as well as a proper number sentence.

Use *Question 5* to guide students through the same procedure for $3\frac{1}{4}$. Remind students to use at most two colors of blocks to represent the mixed numbers. *Question 6* asks students to follow the same directions and find different representations for a whole number. Figure 4 shows three ways to represent the number 2 using pattern blocks: $2 = \frac{4}{2} = 1\frac{4}{4}$.

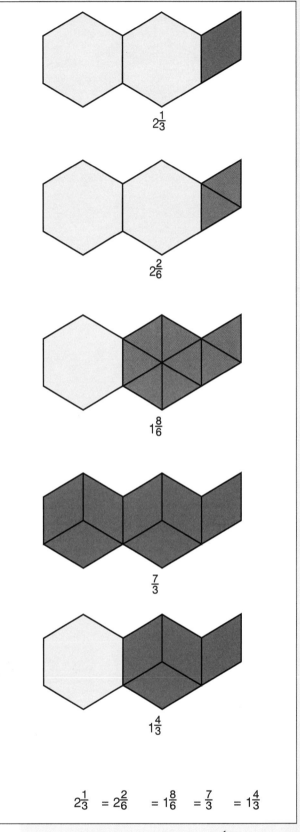

Figure 4: *Three names for 2: $2 = \frac{4}{2} = 1\frac{4}{4}$*

Questions 7–9 ask students to represent improper fractions and mixed numbers with pattern blocks. First, students represent the fraction as it is written in the problem. Then they show the fraction using only two colors and the fewest pieces possible. They write the mixed numbers represented by the pattern blocks using the fewest pieces. Following these restrictions forces students to write mixed numbers with proper fractions in lowest terms. For example, to represent $1\frac{15}{6}$ with two colors and the fewest pieces, we must use yellow and red pieces. As shown in Figure 5, $1\frac{15}{6} = 3\frac{1}{2}$. A different example is shown in the *Student Guide*.

$$2\frac{1}{3} = 2\frac{2}{6} = 1\frac{8}{6} = \frac{7}{3} = 1\frac{4}{3}$$

Figure 3: *Five names for $2\frac{1}{3}$*

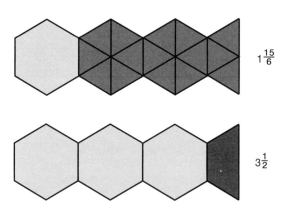

$1\frac{15}{6}$

$3\frac{1}{2}$

Figure 5: $1\frac{15}{6} = 3\frac{1}{2}$

Questions 10–12 provide practice renaming mixed numbers and improper fractions that cannot be modeled with pattern blocks.

Math Facts

DPP Bit A reviews the last six division facts.

Homework and Practice

* The Homework section in the *Student Guide* provides practice renaming mixed numbers. This section also provides practice solving problems involving fractions.

* Assign DPP Challenge B that involves making and understanding scale maps and using ratios to solve problems.

Assessment

* Use the Journal Prompt from Part 1 in the *Unit Resource Guide* to assess students' abilities to estimate sums of fractions.

* Use *Question 1* of the Homework section to assess students' abilities to rename mixed numbers.

* Use the *Observational Assessment Record* to note students' abilities to add mixed numbers.

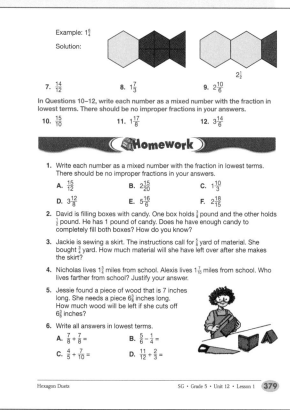

Example: $1\frac{6}{4}$

Solution:

$2\frac{1}{2}$

7. $\frac{14}{12}$ 8. $1\frac{7}{3}$ 9. $2\frac{10}{6}$

In Questions 10–12, write each number as a mixed number with the fraction in lowest terms. There should be no improper fractions in your answers.

10. $\frac{15}{10}$ 11. $1\frac{17}{8}$ 12. $3\frac{14}{6}$

Homework

1. Write each number as a mixed number with the fraction in lowest terms. There should be no improper fractions in your answers.
   A. $\frac{15}{12}$ B. $2\frac{15}{20}$ C. $1\frac{10}{3}$
   D. $3\frac{12}{8}$ E. $5\frac{16}{6}$ F. $2\frac{18}{15}$

2. David is filling boxes with candy. One box holds $\frac{3}{4}$ pound and the other holds $\frac{1}{2}$ pound of candy. He has 1 pound of candy. Does he have enough candy to completely fill both boxes? How do you know?

3. Jackie is sewing a skirt. The instructions call for $\frac{5}{8}$ yard of material. She bought $\frac{3}{4}$ yard. How much material will she have left over after she makes the skirt?

4. Nicholas lives $1\frac{3}{4}$ miles from school. Alexis lives $1\frac{7}{10}$ miles from school. Who lives farther from school? Justify your answer.

5. Jessie found a piece of wood that is 7 inches long. She needs a piece $6\frac{3}{8}$ inches long. How much wood will be left if she cuts off $6\frac{3}{8}$ inches?

6. Write all answers in lowest terms.
   A. $\frac{7}{8} + \frac{7}{8} =$ B. $\frac{5}{6} - \frac{1}{4} =$
   C. $\frac{4}{5} + \frac{7}{10} =$ D. $\frac{11}{12} + \frac{2}{3} =$

Hexagon Duets   SG • Grade 5 • Unit 12 • Lesson 1   **379**

Student Guide - page 379 *(Answers on p. 29)*

At a Glance

Math Facts and Daily Practice and Problems

DPP Bit A reviews the last six division facts. Challenge B involves scale maps and using ratios to solve problems.

Part 1. Playing *Hexagon Duets*

1. Students read and discuss the rules for the game on the *Hexagon Duets* Activity Pages in the *Student Guide.*
2. Students read and discuss the example of a round of play in the *Student Guide* and answer *Questions 1–3.*
3. Students play the game using pattern blocks, a spinner, and the *Hexagon Duets Spinner* Game Page from the *Discovery Assignment Book.*

Part 2. Many Names for Mixed Numbers

1. Students find equivalent representations for mixed numbers using pattern blocks. (*Questions 4–9*)
2. Students find equivalent representations for mixed numbers using pencil and paper. (*Questions 10–12*)

Homework

Assign the Homework section in the *Student Guide.*

Assessment

1. Use the Journal Prompt as an assessment.
2. Use *Question 1* of the Homework section to assess renaming mixed numbers.
3. Use the *Observational Assessment Record* to note students' abilities to add mixed numbers.

Answer Key is on pages 28–29.

Notes:

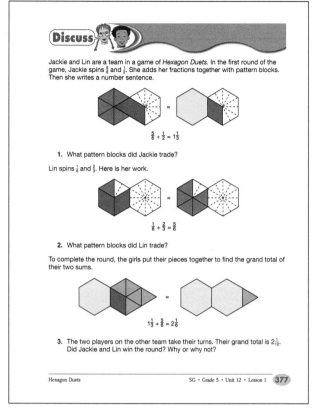

Student Guide - page 377

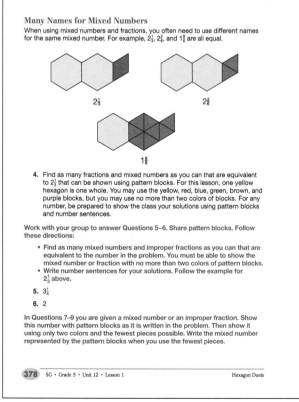

Student Guide - page 378

*Answers and/or discussion are included in the Lesson Guide.

Student Guide (pp. 377–378)

1. Jackie traded 5 green triangles and 1 red trapezoid for 1 yellow hexagon and 1 blue rhombus.

2. Lin traded 1 green triangle and 2 blue rhombuses for 5 green triangles.

3. Yes, $2\frac{1}{6} > 2\frac{1}{12}$.

4. See Figure 3 in Lesson Guide 1.*

5. Answers will vary. Possible solutions include:
$3\frac{1}{4} = 2\frac{5}{4} = 3\frac{3}{12} = \frac{13}{4}$

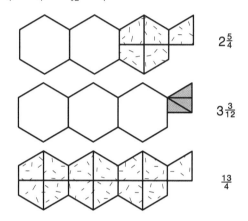

6. See Figure 4 in Lesson Guide 1.*

Student Guide (p. 379)

7. $\frac{14}{12}$  solution: $1\frac{1}{6}$

8. 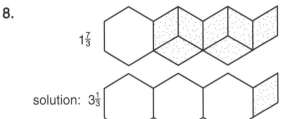 $1\frac{7}{3}$

solution: $3\frac{1}{3}$

9. 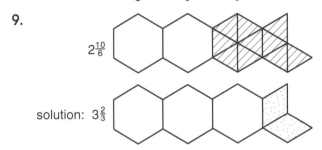 $2\frac{10}{6}$

solution: $3\frac{2}{3}$

10. $1\frac{1}{2}$

11. $3\frac{1}{8}$

12. $5\frac{1}{3}$

Homework

1. A. $1\frac{1}{4}$

B. $2\frac{3}{4}$

C. $4\frac{1}{3}$

D. $4\frac{1}{2}$

E. $7\frac{2}{3}$

F. $3\frac{1}{5}$

2. Yes; the two boxes together hold $\frac{3}{8} + \frac{1}{2} = \frac{7}{8}$ pound of candy. Since David has 1 pound of candy, he has enough candy to fill the two boxes.

3. $\frac{1}{8}$ yard

4. Nicholas. Students' justifications will vary.

5. $\frac{5}{8}$ inch

6. A. $\frac{7}{4}$ or $1\frac{3}{4}$

B. $\frac{7}{12}$

C. $\frac{3}{2}$ or $1\frac{1}{2}$

D. $\frac{19}{12}$ or $1\frac{7}{12}$

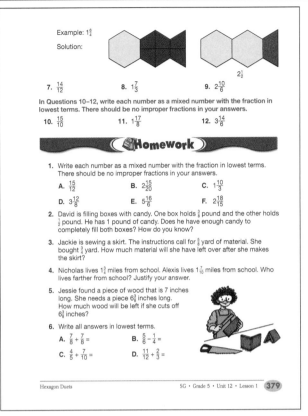

Student Guide - page 379

Adding Mixed Numbers

Lesson Overview

Estimated Class Sessions

1

Students use pattern blocks to model the addition of mixed numbers and develop paper-and-pencil procedures.

Key Content

- Adding mixed numbers using paper and pencil.
- Reducing fractions to lowest terms.
- Estimating sums of mixed numbers.

Homework

1. Assign the homework problems in the *Student Guide*.
2. Assign Parts 1–2 of the Home Practice.

Assessment

Use *Questions 3–4* of the Homework section as an assessment.

Curriculum Sequence

Before This Unit

Students converted improper fractions to mixed numbers in Unit 3 Lesson 2. They reviewed using common denominators to add fractions with paper and pencil in Unit 11 Lesson 6.

Materials List

Supplies and Copies

Student	Teacher
Supplies for Each Student Pair • 1 set of pattern blocks (2–3 yellow hexagons, 6 red trapezoids, 10 blue rhombuses, 10 green triangles, 6 brown trapezoids, 12 purple triangles)	**Supplies** • overhead pattern blocks, optional
Copies	**Copies/Transparencies**

All blackline masters including assessment, transparency, and DPP masters are also on the Teacher Resource CD.

Student Books
Adding Mixed Numbers (*Student Guide* Pages 380–382)

Daily Practice and Problems and Home Practice
DPP items C–D (*Unit Resource Guide* Page 15)
Home Practice Parts 1–2 (*Discovery Assignment Book* Page 189)

Note: Classrooms whose pacing differs significantly from the suggested pacing of the units should use the Math Facts Calendar in Section 4 of the *Facts Resource Guide* to ensure students receive the complete math facts program.

C. Bit: Do You See a Triangle?

(URG p. 15)

In each case, tell whether the given lengths
will make a triangle. Justify your answer.
(*Hint:* Estimation is an appropriate strategy
for solving this problem.)

A. 3 inches, 4 inches, 6 inches
B. $3\frac{1}{2}$ inches, 8 inches, $4\frac{5}{8}$ inches
C. $15\frac{3}{16}$ inches, $7\frac{1}{4}$ inches, $7\frac{3}{8}$ inches

D. Challenge: Making a Quilt

(URG p. 15)

1. Mrs. Sorenson is teaching the students in
   Mr. Moreno's class how to make a patchwork
   quilt. The entire quilt will be a rectangle
   measuring 4 feet by 5 feet. The quilt will
   be made up of individual squares, each
   measuring 6 inches by 6 inches. How many
   individual squares are needed to make the
   quilt? Explain how you solved the problem.

2. There are 22 students in Mr. Moreno's class.
   The students are going to cut the individual
   squares from scraps of material. How many
   individual squares should each student cut
   out to have enough squares for the quilt?

TIMS Tip

Students should work in pairs to share pattern blocks.

Teaching the Activity

Briefly review the addition of fractions by using pattern blocks as a model. Figure 6 shows one way to
add $\frac{2}{3}$ and $\frac{1}{2}$ using pattern blocks. Note that finding
the common denominator (6) is modeled by finding
one color (green) to cover both addends. Other
strategies of combining the blocks are also possible.

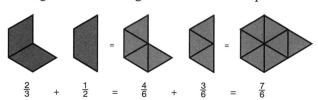

$$\frac{2}{3} \quad + \quad \frac{1}{2} \quad = \quad \frac{4}{6} \quad + \quad \frac{3}{6} \quad = \quad \frac{7}{6}$$

Figure 6: *Finding common denominators using
pattern blocks to find common colors of blocks*

Remind students to check for the reasonableness of
their answers. Ask:

• *Should the answer be more or less than $\frac{1}{2}$?
  More or less than 1?*

Have students use pattern blocks to add mixed
numbers using these examples:

$$2\frac{1}{6} + 1\frac{1}{3}$$

$$1\frac{1}{2} + 2\frac{3}{4}$$

Discuss strategies. Students can find a common denominator by covering all the fractional pieces with pieces of one color. Another strategy for adding $1\frac{1}{2} + 2\frac{3}{4}$ is shown in Figure 7.

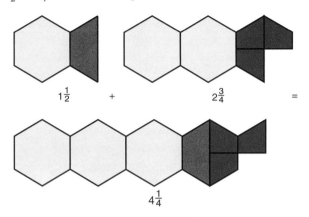

$1\frac{1}{2}$ + $2\frac{3}{4}$ =

$4\frac{1}{4}$

Figure 7: *Adding $1\frac{1}{2} + 2\frac{3}{4}$*

Have students use pencil and paper to do the same problems. Students can rely on skills they have used previously to add fractions. The only new aspect here is that we have wholes as well as fractional pieces. The problem $1\frac{1}{2} + 2\frac{3}{4}$ is discussed in the *Student Guide*. After students share their strategies, they can read the discussion of this problem on the *Adding Mixed Numbers* Activity Pages in the *Student Guide* and compare strategies. Discuss the last step. Since the mixed number $3\frac{5}{4}$ contains an improper fraction, it is rewritten as $4\frac{1}{4}$ ($3\frac{5}{4} = 3 + 1\frac{1}{4} = 4\frac{1}{4}$).

The questions in the Explore section give students practice adding mixed numbers with and without pattern blocks. Students should work on the problems in *Question 1* in pairs using pattern blocks. The problems in *Question 2* cannot be solved using pattern blocks. Use these problems as examples to show students generalized procedures for adding mixed numbers. Students may choose to add the fractions first, then change any improper fractions in the sum to mixed numbers. Or students may choose to change the mixed numbers to improper fractions before they add.

Question 3 asks students to describe a method for adding mixed numbers. No matter what strategy students choose, encourage them to check to see if their answers are reasonable and that there are no improper fractions in their final answers.

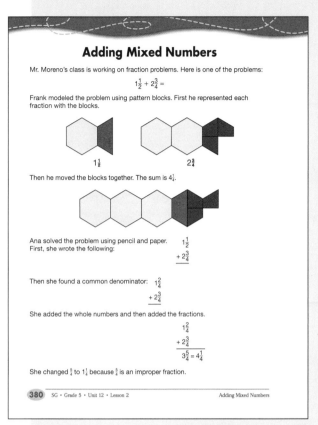

Student Guide - page 380

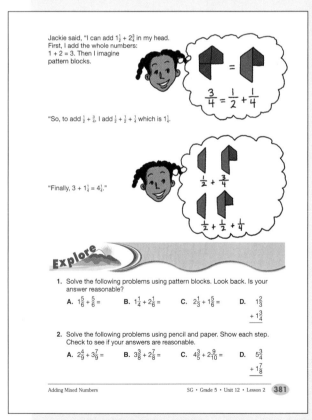

Student Guide - page 381 (Answers on p. 36)

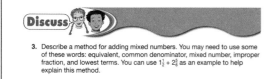

Name _____ Date _____

Unit 12 Home Practice

PART 1 **Multiplication and Division Practice**
Use a paper-and-pencil method to solve the following problems. Write any remainders as fractions in lowest terms.

1. A. $8967 \div 6 =$ B. $5875 \div 50 =$
   C. $246 \times 9 =$ D. $2400 \div 30 =$
   E. $105 \times 4 =$

2. Can you solve any of the above problems using mental math? If so, explain your strategies.

PART 2 **Division Practice**
1. Solve the following problems in your head or with paper and pencil. Write the quotient as a mixed number. Reduce all fractions to lowest terms.
   A. $33 \div 4 =$ B. $76 \div 9 =$ C. $17 \div 2 =$

   D. $108 \div 10 =$ E. $54 \div 7 =$ F. $41 \div 6 =$

   G. $42 \div 8 =$ H. $23 \div 6 =$ I. $67 \div 8 =$

2. Use a calculator to find the answers to the following. Write your answers as mixed numbers. Reduce all fractions to lowest terms.
   A. $1388 \div 16 =$ B. $18,478 \div 24 =$ C. $43,956 \div 32 =$

USING FRACTIONS   DAB • Grade 5 • Unit 12 **189**

Discovery Assignment Book - page 189 *(Answers on p. 37)*

Discuss

3. Describe a method for adding mixed numbers. You may need to use some of these words: equivalent, common denominator, mixed number, improper fraction, and lowest terms. You can use $1\frac{1}{2} + 2\frac{5}{8}$ as an example to help explain this method.

Homework

Solve the following problems using paper and pencil or mental math. Reduce all fractions to lowest terms. Do not leave any improper fractions in your answers.

1. $2 + 4\frac{3}{5} =$ 2. $4\frac{3}{4} + 1\frac{5}{6} =$ 3. $1\frac{7}{10} + 3\frac{1}{2} =$

4. Solve the problem in Question 3 another way. Explain both of your strategies.

5. $5\frac{2}{3} + 3\frac{1}{12} =$ 6. $3\frac{4}{5} + 2\frac{1}{5} =$ 7. $\begin{array}{r} 7\frac{1}{5} \\ + 2\frac{1}{10} \end{array}$ 8. $\begin{array}{r} 4\frac{3}{5} \\ + 5\frac{3}{4} \end{array}$

9. Look back at your answer to Question 8. Is it reasonable? Should it be more than 10 or less than 10? Explain.

10. Lee Yah spent $6\frac{1}{2}$ hours in school and $1\frac{3}{4}$ hours doing her homework. What is the total time she spent at school and on her homework?

11. A recipe calls for $1\frac{1}{3}$ cups of whole wheat flour and $2\frac{3}{4}$ cups of white flour. How many cups of flour are needed?

12. Nicholas checked the odometer in the car when he got a ride to school. His route to school is 1.3 miles. His soccer coach told him that it is a mile and a half from school to the practice field. How far does Nicholas have to walk to get from home to school to soccer practice?

13. A. A customer bought $2\frac{1}{3}$ yards of print material and $2\frac{1}{3}$ yards of solid color material. How many yards did the customer buy?
    B. Both kinds of material cost $3.00 a yard. The customer has $15. Is this enough money to buy the material? Explain.

14. Jessie is making a bird house. She needs 2 boards that measure $1\frac{3}{4}$ feet each and a board that measures $1\frac{1}{2}$ feet long. She has one board that is 4 feet long. Can she cut the 3 shorter boards from the longer one? Why or why not?

382 SG • Grade 5 • Unit 12 • Lesson 2   Adding Mixed Numbers

Student Guide - page 382 *(Answers on p. 36)*

Homework and Practice

- Before assigning the homework, check to see if students are comfortable solving problems written both horizontally and vertically by noting student progress as they work on *Questions 1–2* in the Explore section. Encourage students to use the example problem in the *Student Guide* to help them solve the problems in the Homework section.

- Assign DPP item C. Bit C reviews geometry concepts including side lengths of triangles and requires estimating sums of fractions.

- Assign Parts 1 and 2 of the Home Practice that provide practice with multiplication and division. Students will need a calculator for Part 2.

Answers for Parts 1 and 2 of the Home Practice are in the Answer Key at the end of this lesson and at the end of this unit.

Assessment

Use *Questions 3–4* in the Homework section to assess student abilities to add mixed numbers using more than one strategy and to explain their thinking.

Extension

DPP Challenge D extends students' fluency with geometric concepts involving measurement and area of squares.

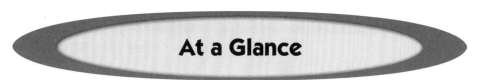

At a Glance

Math Facts and Daily Practice and Problems

DPP Bit C reviews geometry concepts and estimating sums of fractions. DPP item D challenges students to solve a problem about quilts.

Teaching the Activity

1. Briefly review the addition of fractions using pattern blocks and using paper and pencil.
2. Have students use pattern blocks to add mixed numbers, using these examples.

   $2\frac{1}{6} + 1\frac{1}{3}$

   $1\frac{1}{2} + 2\frac{3}{4}$

3. Have students use pencil and paper to do the same problems. Discuss strategies.
4. Students read the discussion on the *Adding Mixed Numbers* Activity Pages in the *Student Guide.*
5. Students practice adding mixed numbers using pattern blocks in **Question 1** and without pattern blocks in **Question 2** of the *Adding Mixed Numbers* Activity Pages in the *Student Guide.*
6. Students articulate a general method for adding mixed numbers. **(Question 3)**

Homework

1. Assign the homework problems in the *Student Guide.*
2. Assign Parts 1–2 of the Home Practice.

Assessment

Use **Questions 3–4** of the Homework section as an assessment.

Extension

Assign DPP Challenge D.

Answer Key is on pages 36–37.

Notes:

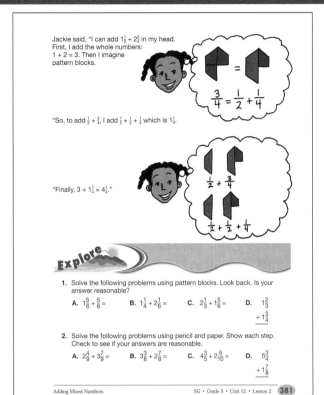

Jackie said, "I can add $1\frac{1}{2} + 2\frac{3}{4}$ in my head. First, I add the whole numbers: $1 + 2 = 3$. Then I imagine pattern blocks."

$$\frac{3}{4} = \frac{1}{2} + \frac{1}{4}$$

"So, to add $\frac{1}{2} + \frac{3}{4}$, I add $\frac{1}{2} + \frac{1}{2} + \frac{1}{4}$ which is $1\frac{1}{4}$."

"Finally, $3 + 1\frac{1}{4} = 4\frac{1}{4}$."

$$\frac{1}{2} + \frac{3}{4}$$
$$\frac{1}{2} + \frac{1}{2} + \frac{1}{4}$$

Explore

1. Solve the following problems using pattern blocks. Look back. Is your answer reasonable?

   A. $1\frac{5}{6} + \frac{5}{6} =$ B. $1\frac{1}{4} + 2\frac{1}{6} =$ C. $2\frac{1}{3} + 1\frac{5}{6} =$ D. $\begin{array}{r} 1\frac{2}{3} \\ + 1\frac{3}{4} \end{array}$

2. Solve the following problems using pencil and paper. Show each step. Check to see if your answers are reasonable.

   A. $2\frac{4}{9} + 3\frac{7}{9} =$ B. $3\frac{3}{8} + 2\frac{7}{8} =$ C. $4\frac{3}{5} + 2\frac{9}{10} =$ D. $\begin{array}{r} 5\frac{3}{4} \\ + 1\frac{7}{8} \end{array}$

Adding Mixed Numbers   SG • Grade 5 • Unit 12 • Lesson 2   **381**

Student Guide - page 381

Discuss

3. Describe a method for adding mixed numbers. You may need to use some of these words: equivalent, common denominator, mixed number, improper fraction, and lowest terms. You can use $1\frac{1}{2} + 2\frac{5}{6}$ as an example to help explain this method.

Homework

Solve the following problems using paper and pencil or mental math. Reduce all fractions to lowest terms. Do not leave any improper fractions in your answers.

1. $2 + 4\frac{3}{5} =$ 2. $4\frac{3}{4} + 1\frac{5}{6} =$ 3. $1\frac{7}{10} + 3\frac{1}{2} =$

4. Solve the problem in Question 3 another way. Explain both of your strategies.

5. $5\frac{2}{3} + 3\frac{1}{12} =$ 6. $3\frac{4}{5} + 2\frac{1}{5} =$ 7. $\begin{array}{r} 7\frac{1}{5} \\ + 2\frac{1}{10} \end{array}$ 8. $\begin{array}{r} 4\frac{3}{5} \\ + 5\frac{3}{4} \end{array}$

9. Look back at your answer to Question 8. Is it reasonable? Should it be more than 10 or less than 10? Explain.

10. Lee Yah spent $6\frac{1}{2}$ hours in school and $1\frac{3}{4}$ hours doing her homework. What is the total time she spent at school and on her homework?

11. A recipe calls for $1\frac{1}{3}$ cups of whole wheat flour and $2\frac{3}{4}$ cups of white flour. How many cups of flour are needed?

12. Nicholas checked the odometer in the car when he got a ride to school. His route to school is 1.3 miles. His soccer coach told him that it is a mile and a half from school to the practice field. How far does Nicholas have to walk to get from home to school to soccer practice?

13. A. A customer bought $2\frac{1}{3}$ yards of print material and $2\frac{3}{4}$ yards of solid color material. How many yards did the customer buy?

    B. Both kinds of material cost $3.00 a yard. The customer has $15. Is this enough money to buy the material? Explain.

14. Jessie is making a bird house. She needs 2 boards that measure $1\frac{3}{4}$ feet each and a board that measures $1\frac{1}{2}$ feet long. She has one board that is 4 feet long. Can she cut the 3 shorter boards from the longer one? Why or why not?

382   SG • Grade 5 • Unit 12 • Lesson 2   Adding Mixed Numbers

Student Guide - page 382

Student Guide (pp. 381–382)

1. A. $2\frac{2}{3}$ B. $3\frac{5}{12}$
   C. $4\frac{1}{6}$ D. $3\frac{5}{12}$

2. A. $6\frac{2}{9}$ B. $6\frac{1}{4}$
   C. $7\frac{1}{2}$ D. $7\frac{5}{8}$

3. Answers will vary. The common denominator for the fractions $\frac{1}{2}$ and $\frac{5}{6}$ is 12. Find equivalent fractions with denominator 12; $\frac{1}{2}$ is equivalent to $\frac{6}{12}$ and $\frac{5}{6}$ is equivalent to $\frac{10}{12}$. Add the whole numbers 1 and 2 to get 3. Now, add the fractions $\frac{6}{12}$ and $\frac{10}{12}$ to get $\frac{16}{12}$. Converting this to mixed numbers, we get $1\frac{4}{12}$. Adding this to 3 we get $4\frac{4}{12}$. Reducing to lowest terms the answer is $4\frac{1}{3}$.

Homework

1. $6\frac{3}{5}$

2. $6\frac{7}{12}$

3. $5\frac{1}{5}$

4. Two possible solutions: $1\frac{7}{10} = 1\frac{7}{10}$, $3\frac{1}{2} = 3\frac{5}{10}$, $4\frac{12}{10} = 5\frac{2}{10} = 5\frac{1}{5}$; Add the whole numbers first: $1 + 3 = 4$. Then, add the fractions. Think of $\frac{7}{10}$ as $\frac{5}{10} + \frac{2}{10}$ or $\frac{1}{2} + \frac{2}{10}$. Then, $\frac{7}{10} + \frac{1}{2} = \frac{1}{2} + \frac{2}{10} + \frac{1}{2}$ or $1\frac{2}{10}$. So, $4 + 1\frac{2}{10} = 5\frac{2}{10} = 5\frac{1}{5}$

5. $8\frac{3}{4}$

6. 6

7. $9\frac{3}{10}$

8. $10\frac{7}{20}$

9. More than 10; the whole numbers add up to 9 and the fractions add up to more than 1.

10. $8\frac{1}{4}$ hours

11. $4\frac{1}{12}$ cups

12. 2.8 miles or $2\frac{4}{5}$ miles

13. A. $5\frac{1}{12}$ yards

    B. No; since the material costs $3.00 per yard, the customer can only buy 5 yards with $15. The total amount of material is more than 5 yards, so the customer won't have enough money.

14. No. $1\frac{3}{4} + 1\frac{3}{4} = 3\frac{1}{2}$ ft. $3\frac{1}{2} + 1\frac{1}{2} > 4$ ft.

Discovery Assignment Book (p. 189)

Home Practice*

Part 1. Multiplication and Division Practice

1. **A.** $1494\frac{1}{2}$

   B. $117\frac{1}{2}$

   C. 2214

   D. 80

   E. 420

2. Answers will vary:
   Possible response for 1E:
   $105 \times 4 = 100 \times 4 + 5 \times 4 = 400 + 20 = 420$

Part 2. Division Practice

1. **A.** $8\frac{1}{4}$ **B.** $8\frac{4}{9}$

   C. $8\frac{1}{2}$ **D.** $10\frac{8}{10} = 10\frac{4}{5}$

   E. $7\frac{5}{7}$ **F.** $6\frac{5}{6}$

   G. $5\frac{2}{8} = 5\frac{1}{4}$ **H.** $3\frac{5}{6}$

   I. $8\frac{3}{8}$

2. **A.** $86\frac{12}{16} = 86\frac{3}{4}$

   B. $769\frac{22}{24} = 769\frac{11}{12}$

   C. $1373\frac{20}{32} = 1373\frac{5}{8}$

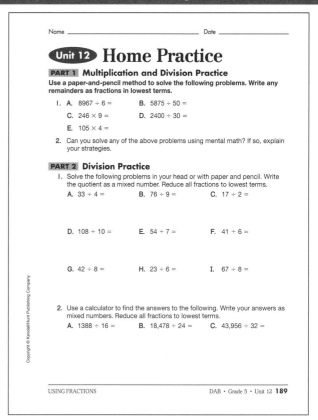

Discovery Assignment Book - page 189

*Answers for all the Home Practice in the *Discovery Assignment Book* are at the end of the unit.

Lesson 3

Fractions of Groups

Lesson Overview

By using diagrams, students find the product of a fraction and a whole number. They also look for patterns in multiplication problems and use the patterns to estimate the size of the products. This lesson helps develop a conceptual understanding of multiplication with fractions and further develops number sense. Students will use paper-and-pencil procedures for multiplication of fractions in Lesson 5.

Key Content

- Multiplying a fraction and a whole number using diagrams.
- Using patterns to build number sense.

Math Facts

DPP Bit E reviews the last six division facts.

Homework

Assign the Homework section in the *Student Guide*.

Assessment

Use *Question 7* in the Homework section as an assessment.

Materials List

Supplies and Copies

Student	Teacher
Supplies for Each Student	**Supplies**
Copies	**Copies/Transparencies**

All blackline masters including assessment, transparency, and DPP masters are also on the Teacher Resource CD.

Student Books
Fractions of Groups (*Student Guide* Pages 383–386)

Daily Practice and Problems and Home Practice
DPP items E–F (*Unit Resource Guide* Page 16)

Note: Classrooms whose pacing differs significantly from the suggested pacing of the units should use the Math Facts Calendar in Section 4 of the *Facts Resource Guide* to ensure students receive the complete math facts program.

Daily Practice and Problems

Suggestions for using the DPPs are on page 43.

E. Bit: Division Facts (URG p. 16)

A. $240 \div 40 =$

B. $4800 \div 60 =$

C. $2800 \div 700 =$

D. $560 \div 70 =$

E. $42{,}000 \div 600 =$

F. $3200 \div 80 =$

F. Task: Practicing the Operations
  (URG p. 16)

Use paper and pencil to solve the following problems. Estimate to be sure your answers are reasonable. For A and B, write your answer (the quotient) as a mixed number. Fractions should be in lowest terms.

1. A. $636 \div 16 =$

   B. $1994 \div 8 =$

   C. $467 \times 8 =$

   D. $37.2 + 125.06 =$

   E. $1045.35 - 76.3 =$

   F. $0.7 \times 85 =$

2. Explain your estimation strategy for 1F.

In previous units, students explored fractions using area models (rectangles on dot paper and pattern blocks) and a number line model (fractohoppers). In this lesson, students work with fractions of sets of discrete objects. For example, students find the fraction of red apples in a box of 12 apples. The whole is a group of 12 discrete objects. The sequence of discussion questions develops the fraction concepts involved in multiplying a fraction and a whole number. Arrays of apples in gift boxes of different sizes provide the context.

Students investigate the concept of a whole in *Questions 1–2.* Just as the size of a fraction using an area model depends on the area of the whole, the size of a fraction of a set of discrete objects depends on the number of objects in the whole set. First, students find the number of apples in two different-sized gift boxes. One-fourth of the apples in a box of 12 apples is three apples *(Question 1A),* while one-fourth of a box of 24 apples is six apples *(Question 1B).*

Question 2 reviews the terms numerator and denominator. For the fraction $\frac{1}{4}$, the 4 in the denominator tells us to divide the 12 apples into four equal groups. The 1 in the numerator tells us we are interested in one of the groups. To know the number of apples in $\frac{1}{4}$ of a box of apples, it is essential to know the number of apples in the whole box *(Question 2C).* To show the difference between the fractions $\frac{1}{4}$ and $\frac{4}{1}$ *(Question 2D),* we can apply the definitions of numerator and denominator to $\frac{4}{1}$. For the fraction $\frac{4}{1}$, the 1 in the denominator tells us that all of the apples in the whole set are in one group. The 4 in the numerator means that we are interested in 4 whole groups, so $\frac{4}{1}$ is equivalent to 4 whole boxes.

Questions 3–5 emphasize the language used in multiplication sentences. A number sentence for "Four groups of 6 apples makes 24 apples in all" is $4 \times 6 = 24$. Similarly, a number sentence for "One-fourth of a group of 24 apples is 6 apples" is $\frac{1}{4} \times 24 = 6$. You may wish to ask students to write number sentences for the following:

- *How many players are on 8 teams of 11 players each?* $(8 \times 11 = 88)$
- *One-half of a class of 22 students goes home for lunch. How many students go home for lunch?* $(\frac{1}{2} \times 22 = 11)$

TIMS Tip

Use *Questions 1–9* on the *Fractions of Groups* Activity Pages in the *Student Guide* to lead the discussion. You may need to provide more examples or further explanation for a particular concept or skill.

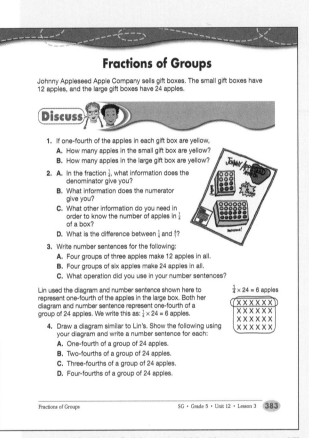

Fractions of Groups

Johnny Appleseed Apple Company sells gift boxes. The small gift boxes have 12 apples, and the large gift boxes have 24 apples.

Discuss

1. If one-fourth of the apples in each gift box are yellow,
   A. How many apples in the small gift box are yellow?
   B. How many apples in the large gift box are yellow?

2. A. In the fraction $\frac{1}{4}$, what information does the denominator give you?
   B. What information does the numerator give you?
   C. What other information do you need in order to know the number of apples in $\frac{1}{4}$ of a box?
   D. What is the difference between $\frac{1}{4}$ and $\frac{4}{1}$?

3. Write number sentences for the following:
   A. Four groups of three apples make 12 apples in all.
   B. Four groups of six apples make 24 apples in all.
   C. What operation did you use in your number sentences?

Lin used the diagram and number sentence shown here to represent one-fourth of the apples in the large box. Both her diagram and number sentence represent one-fourth of a group of 24 apples. We write this as: $\frac{1}{4} \times 24 = 6$ apples.

$\frac{1}{4} \times 24 = 6$ apples

4. Draw a diagram similar to Lin's. Show the following using your diagram and write a number sentence for each:
   A. One-fourth of a group of 24 apples.
   B. Two-fourths of a group of 24 apples.
   C. Three-fourths of a group of 24 apples.
   D. Four-fourths of a group of 24 apples.

Fractions of Groups   SG • Grade 5 • Unit 12 • Lesson 3   **383**

Student Guide - page 383 (Answers on p. 45)

Content Note

Note that while the word "of" often implies multiplication, it is important not to overgeneralize. For example, the problems below use the word "of" but are solved without multiplication:

Six of the students in Mr. Moreno's class are learning to play instruments, and eight of his students are in the chorus. How many are studying music?

If there are 22 students in Mr. Moreno's class, what fraction of the students are learning to play an instrument?

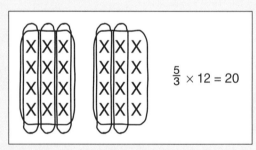

Student Guide - page 384 *(Answers on p. 46)*

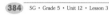

$$\frac{5}{3} \times 12 = 20$$

Figure 9: *A diagram for $\frac{5}{3} \times 12 = 20$*

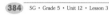

Journal Prompt

If you multiply a fraction and a whole number, when will the product be greater than the whole number? When will the product be less than the whole number?

Questions 6–7 develop students' number sense so they will be able to estimate the product of a fraction and a whole number. Students use diagrams to complete the table in Figure 8.

Multiplication Number Sentences
$\frac{1}{3} \times 12 = 4$
$\frac{2}{3} \times 12 = 8$
$\frac{3}{3} \times 12 = 12$
$\frac{4}{3} \times 12 = 16$
$\frac{5}{3} \times 12 = 20$
$\frac{6}{3} \times 12 = 24$

Figure 8: *Completed table for Question 6*

A diagram is used in the *Student Guide* to solve the problem $\frac{4}{3} \times 12 = 16$. Ask students if they can solve the problem another way. They may see that since $\frac{4}{3}$ equals $1\frac{1}{3}$, the problem can be rewritten as $1\frac{1}{3} \times 12$. Remind students that $1\frac{1}{3}$ can be thought of as 1 and $\frac{1}{3}$ or $1 + \frac{1}{3}$. Using the context of the apple gift boxes, we can find the number of apples in one whole box (12) and the number of apples in $\frac{1}{3}$ of a box (4) and reason that one and one-third boxes of apples is $12 + 4$ or 16 apples.

To complete the row for $\frac{5}{3} \times 12$, students can draw a diagram similar to the one in Figure 9 that shows two whole sets of 12 apples. Each set is divided into three groups, and five of the groups are circled, so $\frac{5}{3} \times 12 = 20$.

Question 7A asks students to look for patterns in the table. Possible student responses include:

- As the fraction gets larger, the product gets larger.
- You can find the products by skip counting by fours since $\frac{1}{3}$ of 12 is 4.
- When the fraction is less than one, the product is less than 12.
- When the fraction is greater than one, the product is greater than 12.

Question 7C asks students when the product of a fraction and 12 is equal to 12. The product is equal to 12 when the fraction is $\frac{3}{3}$ or 1. This is because multiplying a number by one results in the same number.

Math Facts

DPP item E reviews the last six division facts using multiples of 10.

Homework and Practice

- The Homework section in the *Student Guide* reviews the concepts developed in the discussion questions. Encourage students to use both diagrams and number sentences as part of their solutions.

- Assign DPP Task F that reviews computation.

Assessment

Use *Question 7* in the Homework section to assess students' understanding of the concepts and their abilities to find the product of a fraction and a whole number.

---

8. Draw a diagram and write a number sentence for each problem.

   A. $\frac{1}{4} \times 12$ B. $\frac{2}{4} \times 12$ C. $\frac{3}{4} \times 12$

   D. $\frac{4}{4} \times 12$ E. $\frac{5}{4} \times 12$ F. $\frac{6}{4} \times 12$

Homework

Solve the following problems. Draw a diagram and write a number sentence for each problem. Follow the example.

Example: Edward gave $\frac{2}{3}$ of a small box of apples to his grandmother. How many apples did he give her?

$\frac{2}{3} \times 12 = 8$

Remember, there are 12 apples in a small box and 24 apples in a large box.

1. A. One-half of the apples in the small box of apples are red. How many are red?
   B. One-fourth of the apples in the small box are green. How many are green?

2. Nila's family received a large box of apples.
   A. Nila ate $\frac{1}{8}$ of the apples. How many apples did Nila eat?
   B. Nila's father took $\frac{2}{8}$ of the apples to work to share with his co-workers. How many apples did he take to work?

3. For each problem, decide how many apples each person ate.
   A. Manny ate $\frac{1}{3}$ of a large box of apples.
   B. Blanca ate $\frac{1}{8}$ of the apples in a large box.
   C. Michael ate $\frac{3}{4}$ of the apples in a small box.
   D. Romesh ate $\frac{5}{8}$ of the apples in a small box.

Student Guide - page 385 *(Answers on p. 47)*

---

4. Muffy's Muffins are sold in packages of eight. Complete the following table:

Multiplication Number Sentences
$\frac{1}{4} \times 8 = 2$
$\frac{2}{4} \times 8 =$
$\frac{3}{4} \times 8 =$
$\frac{4}{4} \times 8 =$
$\frac{5}{4} \times 8 =$
$\frac{6}{4} \times 8 =$

5. A. Describe the patterns you see in the table.
   B. When is the product equal to the number of muffins in the whole package? Why?
   C. When is the product less than the number of muffins in the whole package? Why?
   D. When is the product more than the number of muffins in the whole package? Why?
   E. What is another name for $\frac{2}{4}$? Rewrite a number sentence from your chart using this name.

6. Lee Yah's friends ate $1\frac{1}{2}$ packages of Muffy's Muffins. How many muffins did they eat?

7. Solve the following problems.

   A. $\frac{1}{10} \times 20 =$ B. $\frac{1}{5} \times 20 =$

   C. $\frac{1}{4} \times 20 =$ D. $\frac{1}{2} \times 20 =$

   E. $\frac{3}{5} \times 20 =$ F. $\frac{3}{4} \times 20 =$

   G. $\frac{9}{10} \times 20 =$ H. $1\frac{1}{2} \times 20 =$

Student Guide - page 386 *(Answers on p. 48)*

Math Facts and Daily Practice and Problems

DPP Bit E reviews the last six division facts. Task F reviews computation with whole numbers and decimals.

Teaching the Activity

Use *Questions 1–8* in the *Student Guide* to lead a class discussion that explores the concepts needed to multiply a fraction and a whole number.

Homework

Assign the Homework section in the *Student Guide.*

Assessment

Use *Question 7* in the Homework section as an assessment.

Answer Key is on pages 45–48.

Notes:

Student Guide (p. 383)

1.* **A.** 3 apples

B. 6 apples

2.* **A.** The 4 in the denominator tells us to divide the whole into 4 equal groups.

B. The 1 in the numerator tells us that we are interested in 1 of the 4 groups.

C. The number of apples in a whole box.

D. $\frac{1}{4}$ means that the whole set is divided into 4 groups and we are interested in one of these groups. $\frac{4}{1}$ means that the whole set is one group and we are interested in 4 of these groups which is the same as 4 whole sets.

3. **A.** $4 \times 3 = 12$ apples

B. $4 \times 6 = 24$ apples*

C. Multiplication

4. **A.** 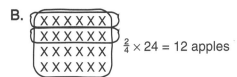 $\frac{1}{4} \times 24 = 6$ apples

B. 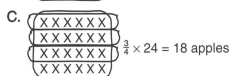 $\frac{2}{4} \times 24 = 12$ apples

C.  $\frac{3}{4} \times 24 = 18$ apples

D. $\frac{4}{4} \times 24 = 24$ apples

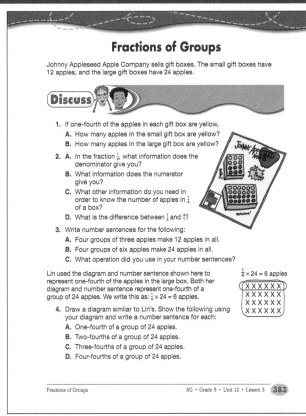

Student Guide - page 383

*Answers and/or discussion are included in the Lesson Guide.

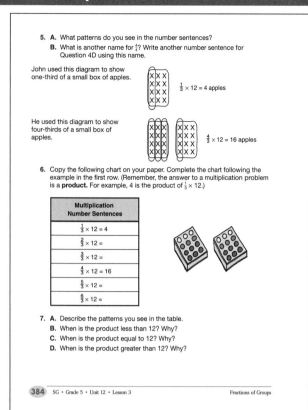

Student Guide - page 384

Student Guide (p. 384)

5. A. All the number sentences show the multiplication of a fraction times 24. The fraction increases by $\frac{1}{4}$ each time. The product increases by 6. You can get the products by skip counting by 6.

B. 1; $1 \times 24 = 24$ apples

6.*

Multiplication Number Sentences
$\frac{1}{3} \times 12 = 4$
$\frac{2}{3} \times 12 = 8$
$\frac{3}{3} \times 12 = 12$
$\frac{4}{3} \times 12 = 16$
$\frac{5}{3} \times 12 = 20$
$\frac{6}{3} \times 12 = 24$

7. A. See possible answers in Lesson Guide 3. Multiplying 12 by a fraction less than one is the same as finding a fractional part of 12. So, the product will be less than 12.*

B. The product is less than 12 when the fraction is less than 1.

C. The product is equal to 12 when the fraction is $\frac{3}{3}$; $\frac{3}{3} = 1$ and multiplying a number by 1 gives the same number.*

D. The product is greater than 12 when the fraction is greater than 1. Multiplying a number by a fraction greater than one means that you have more than one group of 12, so the product will be greater than 12.

*Answers and/or discussion are included in the Lesson Guide.

Student Guide (p. 385)

8. A. 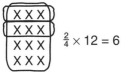 $\frac{1}{4} \times 12 = 3$

B.  $\frac{2}{4} \times 12 = 6$

C. 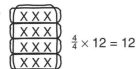 $\frac{3}{4} \times 12 = 9$

D. $\frac{4}{4} \times 12 = 12$

E. $\frac{5}{4} \times 12 = 15$

F. 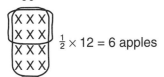 $\frac{6}{4} \times 12 = 18$

Homework

1. A. 6 apples

 $\frac{1}{2} \times 12 = 6$ apples

B. 3 apples

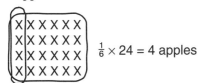 $\frac{1}{4} \times 12 = 3$ apples

2. A. 4 apples

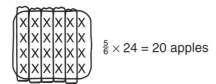 $\frac{1}{6} \times 24 = 4$ apples

B. 20 apples

$\frac{5}{6} \times 24 = 20$ apples

8. Draw a diagram and write a number sentence for each problem.
  A. $\frac{1}{4} \times 12$ **B.** $\frac{2}{4} \times 12$ **C.** $\frac{3}{4} \times 12$
  D. $\frac{4}{4} \times 12$ **E.** $\frac{5}{4} \times 12$ **F.** $\frac{6}{4} \times 12$

 Homework

Solve the following problems. Draw a diagram and write a number sentence for each problem. Follow the example.

Example: Edward gave $\frac{2}{3}$ of a small box of apples to his grandmother. How many apples did he give her?

$\frac{2}{3} \times 12 = 8$

Remember, there are 12 apples in a small box and 24 apples in a large box.

1. A. One-half of the apples in the small box of apples are red. How many are red?
  B. One-fourth of the apples in the small box are green. How many are green?

2. Nila's family received a large box of apples.
  A. Nila ate $\frac{1}{6}$ of the apples. How many apples did Nila eat?
  B. Nila's father took $\frac{5}{6}$ of the apples to work to share with his co-workers. How many apples did he take to work?

3. For each problem, decide how many apples each person ate.
  A. Manny ate $\frac{1}{3}$ of a large box of apples.
  B. Blanca ate $\frac{1}{8}$ of the apples in a large box.
  C. Michael ate $\frac{3}{4}$ of the apples in a small box.
  D. Romesh ate $\frac{5}{6}$ of the apples in a small box.

Fractions of Groups   SG • Grade 5 • Unit 12 • Lesson 3   385

Student Guide - page 385

3. A. 8 apples

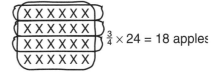 $\frac{1}{3} \times 24 = 8$ apples

B. 3 apples

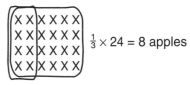 $\frac{1}{8} \times 24 = 3$ apples

C. 18 apples

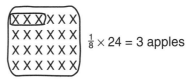 $\frac{3}{4} \times 24 = 18$ apples

D. 20 apples

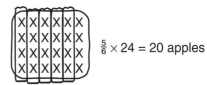 $\frac{5}{6} \times 24 = 20$ apples

4. Muffy's Muffins are sold in packages of eight. Complete the following table:

Multiplication Number Sentences
$\frac{1}{4} \times 8 = 2$
$\frac{2}{4} \times 8 =$
$\frac{3}{4} \times 8 =$
$\frac{4}{4} \times 8 =$
$\frac{5}{4} \times 8 =$
$\frac{6}{4} \times 8 =$

5. A. Describe the patterns you see in the table.
   B. When is the product equal to the number of muffins in the whole package? Why?
   C. When is the product less than the number of muffins in the whole package? Why?
   D. When is the product more than the number of muffins in the whole package? Why?
   E. What is another name for $\frac{2}{4}$? Rewrite a number sentence from your chart using this name.

6. Lee Yah's friends ate $1\frac{1}{2}$ packages of Muffy's Muffins. How many muffins did they eat?

7. Solve the following problems.
   A. $\frac{1}{10} \times 20 =$ **B.** $\frac{1}{5} \times 20 =$
   C. $\frac{1}{4} \times 20 =$ **D.** $\frac{1}{2} \times 20 =$
   E. $\frac{3}{5} \times 20 =$ **F.** $\frac{3}{4} \times 20 =$
   G. $\frac{9}{10} \times 20 =$ **H.** $1\frac{1}{2} \times 20 =$

Student Guide **- page 386**

Student Guide (p. 386)

4.

Multiplication Number Sentences
$\frac{1}{4} \times 8 = 2$
$\frac{2}{4} \times 8 = 4$
$\frac{3}{4} \times 8 = 6$
$\frac{4}{4} \times 8 = 8$
$\frac{5}{4} \times 8 = 10$
$\frac{6}{4} \times 8 = 12$

5. A. Answers will vary. As the fraction gets larger, the product gets larger. You can find products by skip counting by 2 because $\frac{1}{4} \times 8 = 2$.

   B. The product is equal to the number of muffins in the whole package when the fraction is $\frac{4}{4}$; $\frac{4}{4} = 1$, and when a number is multiplied by 1 the product is the same number.

   C. The product is less than the number of muffins in the whole package when the fraction is less than 1. When the number of muffins is multiplied by a fraction less than 1, you are finding a part of the whole package.

   D. The product is more than the number of muffins in the whole package when the fraction is greater than 1. When the number is multiplied by a fraction greater than 1, the product is more than one whole package.

   E. $\frac{1}{2}$; $\frac{1}{2} \times 8 = 4$

6. 12 muffins

7. A. 2
   B. 4
   C. 5
   D. 10
   E. 12
   F. 15
   G. 18
   H. 30

Lesson 4

Multiplication of Fractions

Estimated Class Sessions

1

Lesson Overview

Students use pattern blocks to explore multiplication of fractions. First they model multiplying a fraction times a whole number. Then they model multiplying two fractions. Paper-and-pencil procedures are developed in Lesson 5.

Key Content

- Multiplying a fraction times a whole number using pattern blocks.
- Multiplying a fraction times a fraction using pattern blocks.
- Estimating products of fractions.

Math Facts

DPP Bit G reviews the last six facts.

Homework

Assign the Homework section in the *Student Guide*.

Assessment

1. Use DPP Task H as a quiz to assess students' abilities to add mixed numbers.
2. Check students' homework for their abilities to represent fractions using pattern blocks and number sentences.

Materials List

Supplies and Copies

Student	Teacher
Supplies for Each Student Pair • 1 set of pattern blocks (2–3 yellow hexagons, 6 red trapezoids, 10 blue rhombuses, 10 green triangles, 6 brown trapezoids, 12 purple triangles)	**Supplies** • overhead pattern blocks, optional
Copies	**Copies/Transparencies** • 1 transparency of *Pattern Block Record Sheet,* optional (*Discovery Assignment Book* Pages 195–197)

All blackline masters including assessment, transparency, and DPP masters are also on the Teacher Resource CD.

Student Books

Multiplication of Fractions (*Student Guide* Pages 387–389)
Pattern Block Record Sheet (*Discovery Assignment Book* Pages 195–197)

Daily Practice and Problems and Home Practice

DPP items G–H (*Unit Resource Guide* Page 17)

Note: Classrooms whose pacing differs significantly from the suggested pacing of the units should use the Math Facts Calendar in Section 4 of the *Facts Resource Guide* to ensure students receive the complete math facts program.

Daily Practice and Problems

Suggestions for using the DPPs are on page 56.

6. Bit: Division Facts (URG p. 17)

Find the number n that makes each sentence true.

A. $42 \div 7 = n$ B. $320 \div 4 = n$

C. $56 \div n = 7$ D. $28 \div n = 7$

E. $n \div 6 = 4$ F. $n \div 8 = 6$

H. Task: Adding Mixed Numbers (URG p. 17)

Use paper and pencil to solve the following problems. Write all fractions in lowest terms. Estimate to see if your answers are reasonable.

A. $8\frac{7}{10} + 2\frac{1}{10} =$

B. $2\frac{5}{9} + 3\frac{1}{3} =$

C. $3\frac{1}{12} + 4\frac{3}{8} =$

D. $5\frac{5}{6} + 2\frac{1}{2} =$

E. $5\frac{7}{10} + 2\frac{3}{5} =$

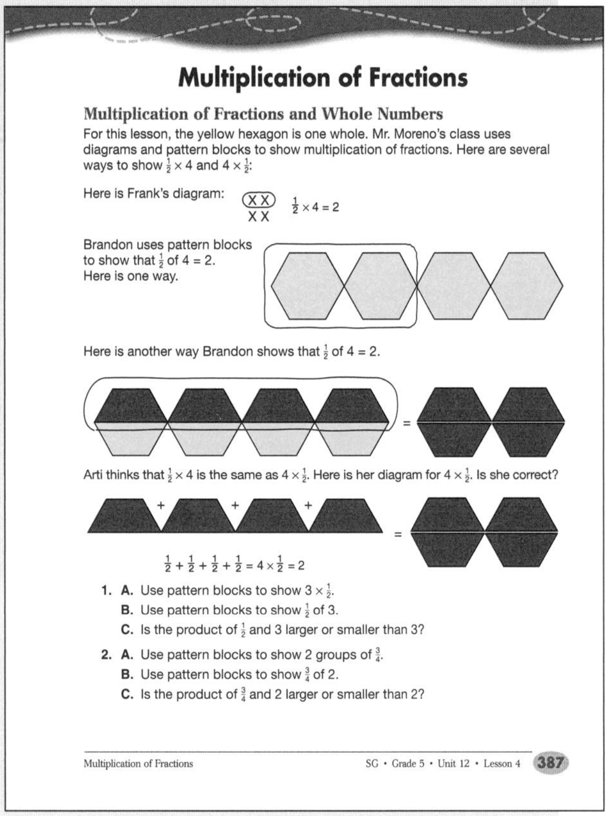

Multiplication of Fractions

Multiplication of Fractions and Whole Numbers

For this lesson, the yellow hexagon is one whole. Mr. Moreno's class uses diagrams and pattern blocks to show multiplication of fractions. Here are several ways to show $\frac{1}{2} \times 4$ and $4 \times \frac{1}{2}$:

Here is Frank's diagram: XX XX $\frac{1}{2} \times 4 = 2$

Brandon uses pattern blocks to show that $\frac{1}{2}$ of 4 = 2. Here is one way.

Here is another way Brandon shows that $\frac{1}{2}$ of 4 = 2.

Arti thinks that $\frac{1}{2} \times 4$ is the same as $4 \times \frac{1}{2}$. Here is her diagram for $4 \times \frac{1}{2}$. Is she correct?

$\frac{1}{2} + \frac{1}{2} + \frac{1}{2} + \frac{1}{2} = 4 \times \frac{1}{2} = 2$

1. **A.** Use pattern blocks to show $3 \times \frac{1}{2}$.
   B. Use pattern blocks to show $\frac{1}{2}$ of 3.
   C. Is the product of $\frac{1}{2}$ and 3 larger or smaller than 3?
2. **A.** Use pattern blocks to show 2 groups of $\frac{3}{4}$.
   B. Use pattern blocks to show $\frac{3}{4}$ of 2.
   C. Is the product of $\frac{3}{4}$ and 2 larger or smaller than 2?

Multiplication of Fractions SG • Grade 5 • Unit 12 • Lesson 4 387

***Student Guide* - page 387** *(Answers on p. 58)*

Teaching the Activity

Part 1 Multiplication of Fractions and Whole Numbers

Begin the lesson by reading and discussing the Multiplication of Fractions and Whole Numbers section on the *Multiplication of Fractions* Activity Pages in the *Student Guide.* The first page shows several ways to represent the multiplication problem $\frac{1}{2} \times 4$. The first diagram uses arrays similar to those in Lesson 3. The second diagram shows two different ways to model $\frac{1}{2}$ of 4 using pattern blocks. (See Figures 10 and 11.) As you discuss the examples in the *Student Guide,* show the examples on the overhead projector using overhead pattern blocks. Remind students that $\frac{1}{2}$ of 4 can be interpreted as $\frac{1}{2} \times 4$.

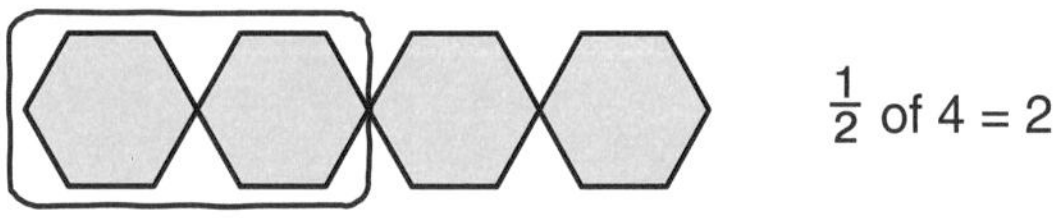

Figure 10: *One way to show $\frac{1}{2} \times 4$ using pattern blocks*

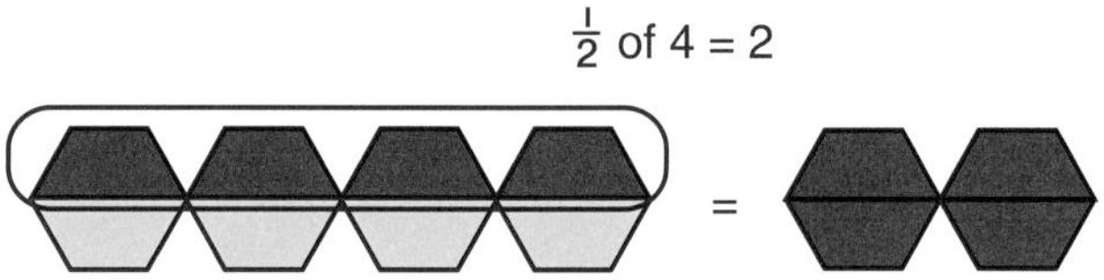

Figure 11: *Another way to show $\frac{1}{2} \times 4$ using pattern blocks*

One way to demonstrate the example in Figure 11 is to cover the top half of 4 yellow hexagons with 4 red trapezoids. Then, rearrange the 4 red trapezoids as shown to represent 2 wholes.

Finally, $\frac{1}{2} \times 4$ is compared to $4 \times \frac{1}{2}$. Students should remember that changing the order of the factors in a multiplication problem does not change the result. Ask students for examples of turnaround facts using whole numbers (e.g., 7×8 and 8×7 are turnaround facts). Pattern blocks are used to show $4 \times \frac{1}{2}$ as repeated addition as shown in Figure 12. So, $\frac{1}{2} \times 4 = 4 \times \frac{1}{2} = 2$.

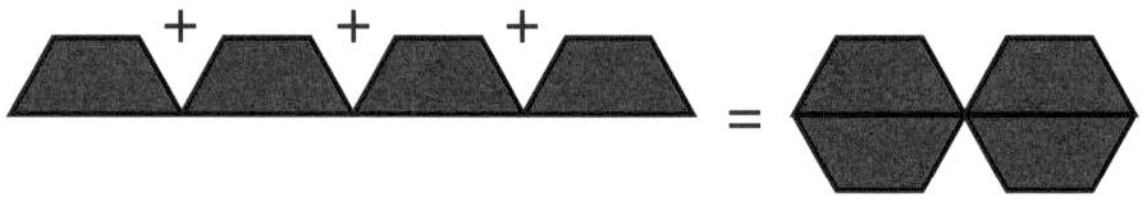

Figure 12: $4 \times \frac{1}{2} = \frac{1}{2} + \frac{1}{2} + \frac{1}{2} + \frac{1}{2} = 2$

Use *Questions 1–7* to lead a class discussion. Ask students to work in pairs to model the multiplication problems in the questions and report their results to the class. Figure 13 shows possible solutions to *Question 1.* To answer *Question 1A,* students can use repeated addition to show $3 \times \frac{1}{2}$ as $\frac{1}{2} + \frac{1}{2} + \frac{1}{2} = \frac{3}{2}$ or $1\frac{1}{2}$. To show $\frac{1}{2}$ of 3 in *Question 1B,* they start with three hexagons and then show that one-half of the 3 hexagons is $1\frac{1}{2}$ hexagons. Students should see that $\frac{1}{2}$ of 3 will be less than 3 since we are finding part of 3 *(Question 1C).*

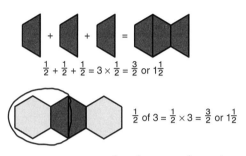

$$\frac{1}{2} + \frac{1}{2} + \frac{1}{2} = 3 \times \frac{1}{2} = \frac{3}{2} \text{ or } 1\frac{1}{2}$$

$$\frac{1}{2} \text{ of } 3 = \frac{1}{2} \times 3 = \frac{3}{2} \text{ or } 1\frac{1}{2}$$

Figure 13: $3 \times \frac{1}{2} = \frac{1}{2} \times 3 = \frac{3}{2}$ or $1\frac{1}{2}$

Questions 2A–2B ask students to show 2 groups of $\frac{3}{4}$ and to compare the result to $\frac{3}{4}$ of 2. When students are working on $\frac{3}{4}$ of 2, remind them to start with 2 yellow hexagons and then show $\frac{3}{4}$ of the 2 hexagons. See Figure 14.

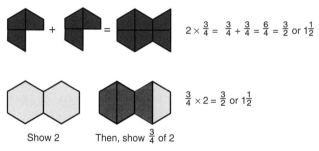

$$2 \times \frac{3}{4} = \frac{3}{4} + \frac{3}{4} = \frac{6}{4} = \frac{3}{2} \text{ or } 1\frac{1}{2}$$

$$\frac{3}{4} \times 2 = \frac{3}{2} \text{ or } 1\frac{1}{2}$$

Show 2   Then, show $\frac{3}{4}$ of 2

Figure 14: $2 \times \frac{3}{4} = \frac{3}{4} \times 2 = \frac{6}{4} = \frac{3}{2}$

Question 2C asks students to look back at their answers and decide if the product is more or less than 2. Encourage students to think about the size of the product. Finding $\frac{3}{4}$ of 2 means finding a part of 2, so the product will be smaller than 2. At the same time we know that the answer will be greater than $\frac{3}{4}$ because twice $\frac{3}{4}$ ($\frac{3}{4} + \frac{3}{4}$) will be greater than $\frac{3}{4}$.

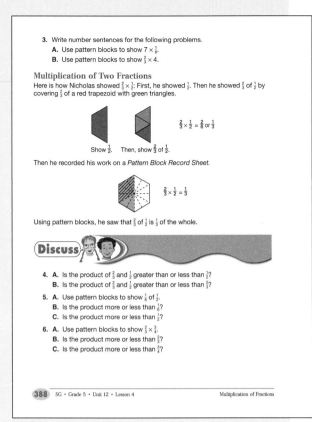
Part 2 Multiplication of Two Fractions

The second part of the lesson extends the use of pattern blocks to modeling the multiplication of a fraction times a fraction. To show $\frac{2}{3} \times \frac{1}{2}$ using pattern blocks, first show $\frac{1}{2}$. Then, find $\frac{2}{3}$ of $\frac{1}{2}$. One-half of a whole (a yellow hexagon) is a red trapezoid. Two-thirds of a red trapezoid can be shown as two green triangles ($\frac{2}{6}$ of a yellow hexagon) or as one blue rhombus ($\frac{1}{3}$ of a yellow hexagon). (See Figure 15.)

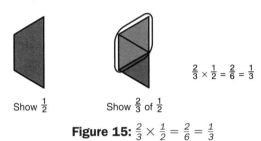

Show $\frac{1}{2}$ Show $\frac{2}{3}$ of $\frac{1}{2}$

$\frac{2}{3} \times \frac{1}{2} = \frac{2}{6} = \frac{1}{3}$

Figure 15: $\frac{2}{3} \times \frac{1}{2} = \frac{2}{6} = \frac{1}{3}$

Question 4 asks students to consider the size of the product. The product of $\frac{2}{3} \times \frac{1}{2}$ is $\frac{1}{3}$. One-third is less than $\frac{1}{2}$ and also less than $\frac{2}{3}$ since we are finding a part of a fraction. Encourage students to think about the equivalent problem $\frac{1}{2}$ of $\frac{2}{3}$. One-half of two of anything is one of those things, so $\frac{1}{2}$ of $\frac{2}{3}$ is $\frac{1}{3}$.

Question 5 is similar to the example. Use pattern blocks on the overhead to help students get started. To show $\frac{1}{6}$ of $\frac{1}{2}$, begin with a red trapezoid to show $\frac{1}{2}$. Then, ask how they can show $\frac{1}{6}$ of $\frac{1}{2}$. Since 6 purple triangles fit on a red trapezoid, one purple triangle, or $\frac{1}{12}$ of a whole hexagon, is $\frac{1}{6}$ of $\frac{1}{2}$. See Figure 16. You may need to emphasize that the product of $\frac{1}{6} \times \frac{1}{2}$ is $\frac{1}{12}$ of the whole. Encourage students to look back at the result. The answer is less than $\frac{1}{2}$ because we are finding a part of $\frac{1}{2}$. Since we know that $\frac{1}{6} \times \frac{1}{2} = \frac{1}{2} \times \frac{1}{6}$, the answer will also be less than $\frac{1}{6}$ because we are finding a part of $\frac{1}{6}$.

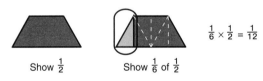

Show $\frac{1}{2}$ Show $\frac{1}{6}$ of $\frac{1}{2}$

$\frac{1}{6} \times \frac{1}{2} = \frac{1}{12}$

Figure 16: $\frac{1}{6} \times \frac{1}{2} = \frac{1}{12}$

One strategy for solving **Question 6** is shown in Figure 17. As students work, they may notice that it is possible to multiply numerators and denominators to find the product before giving the answer in lowest terms. Lesson 5 is designed to develop this procedure. At this time, encourage them to work more problems using pattern blocks to see if the procedure works with other problems.

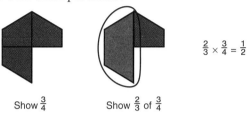

Show $\frac{3}{4}$ Show $\frac{2}{3}$ of $\frac{3}{4}$

$\frac{2}{3} \times \frac{3}{4} = \frac{1}{2}$

Figure 17: $\frac{2}{3} \times \frac{3}{4} = \frac{6}{12} = \frac{1}{2}$

Question 7 prepares students for the homework assignment. They must first estimate a product, solve the problem, write a number sentence, and then record their work on a *Pattern Block Record Sheet* Activity Page from the *Discovery Assignment Book*. For example, the problem in **Question 7B** is $\frac{1}{3} \times \frac{1}{4}$. Students can first estimate that the answer will be less than $\frac{1}{4}$, model the problem with pattern blocks, then record the solution on a *Pattern Block Record Sheet*. To estimate the answer to $8 \times \frac{1}{6}$ **(Question 7D),** we can say that since $\frac{6}{6}$ is equal to 1, $8 \times \frac{1}{6}$ will be greater than 1. The solutions to **Questions 7A–7D** are shown in Figure 18.

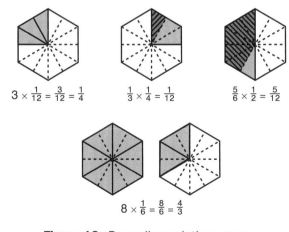

$3 \times \frac{1}{12} = \frac{3}{12} = \frac{1}{4}$ $\frac{1}{3} \times \frac{1}{4} = \frac{1}{12}$ $\frac{5}{6} \times \frac{1}{2} = \frac{5}{12}$

$8 \times \frac{1}{6} = \frac{8}{6} = \frac{4}{3}$

Figure 18: *Recording solutions on a* Pattern Block Record Sheet

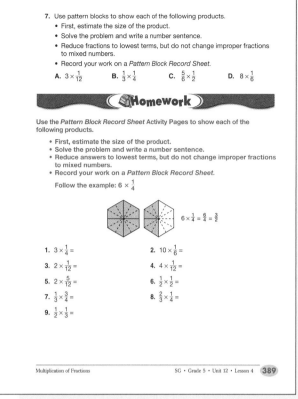

7. Use pattern blocks to show each of the following products.
   • First, estimate the size of the product.
   • Solve the problem and write a number sentence.
   • Reduce fractions to lowest terms, but do not change improper fractions to mixed numbers.
   • Record your work on a *Pattern Block Record Sheet*.
   A. $3 \times \frac{1}{12}$ **B.** $\frac{1}{3} \times \frac{1}{4}$ **C.** $\frac{5}{6} \times \frac{1}{2}$ **D.** $8 \times \frac{1}{6}$

Homework

Use the *Pattern Block Record Sheet* Activity Pages to show each of the following products.
   • First, estimate the size of the product.
   • Solve the problem and write a number sentence.
   • Reduce answers to lowest terms, but do not change improper fractions to mixed numbers.
   • Record your work on a *Pattern Block Record Sheet*.

Follow the example: $6 \times \frac{1}{4}$

$6 \times \frac{1}{4} = \frac{6}{4} = \frac{3}{2}$

1. $3 \times \frac{1}{4} =$ 2. $10 \times \frac{1}{6} =$
3. $2 \times \frac{1}{12} =$ 4. $4 \times \frac{1}{12} =$
5. $2 \times \frac{5}{12} =$ 6. $\frac{1}{2} \times \frac{1}{2} =$
7. $\frac{1}{3} \times \frac{3}{4} =$ 8. $\frac{2}{3} \times \frac{1}{4} =$
9. $\frac{1}{2} \times \frac{1}{3} =$

Multiplication of Fractions   SG • Grade 5 • Unit 12 • Lesson 4   **389**

Student Guide - page 389 (Answers on pp. 59–60)

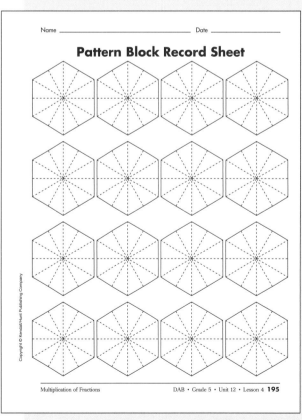

Name _____ Date _____

Pattern Block Record Sheet

Multiplication of Fractions   DAB • Grade 5 • Unit 12 • Lesson 4 **195**

Discovery Assignment Book - page 195

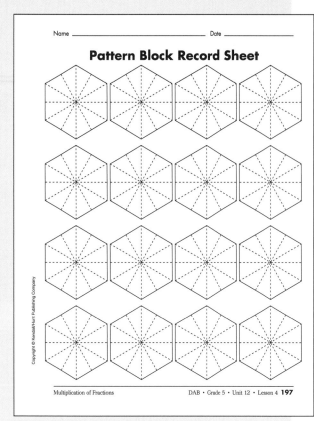

Name _____ Date _____

Pattern Block Record Sheet

Multiplication of Fractions   DAB • Grade 5 • Unit 12 • Lesson 4 **197**

Discovery Assignment Book - page 197

Math Facts

DPP Bit G reviews the last six division facts using variables.

Homework and Practice

Assign the Homework section in the *Student Guide,* which is similar to Discussion *Question 7.* Students will need the *Pattern Block Record Sheet* Activity Pages from the *Discovery Assignment Book* to record their work.

Assessment

- Check the homework problems for students' abilities to represent the solutions to the problems using pattern blocks and number sentences.
- Use DPP Task H to assess students' abilities to add mixed numbers and write sums in lowest terms.

Estimated Class Sessions

1

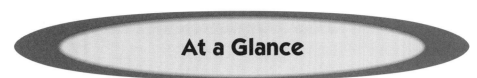

At a Glance

Math Facts and Daily Practice and Problems

DPP Bit G reviews the last six facts. Task H includes problems in adding mixed numbers.

Part 1. Multiplication of Fractions and Whole Numbers

1. Students read and study the examples in the *Student Guide.* Model the examples on the overhead using overhead pattern blocks.
2. Use *Questions 1–3* to lead a class discussion in which students use pattern blocks to model multiplying a fraction times a whole number.

Part 2. Multiplication of Two Fractions

1. Continue the class discussion using *Questions 4–6.* Students use pattern blocks to find the product of two fractions.
2. To answer *Question 7,* students estimate the size of the product, find the product of two fractions using pattern blocks, write a number sentence, then record their work on a *Pattern Block Record Sheet* from the *Discovery Assignment Book.*

Homework

Assign the Homework section in the *Student Guide.*

Assessment

1. Use DPP Task H as a quiz to assess students' abilities to add mixed numbers.
2. Check students' homework for their abilities to represent fractions using pattern blocks and number sentences.

Answer Key is on pages 58–60.

Notes:

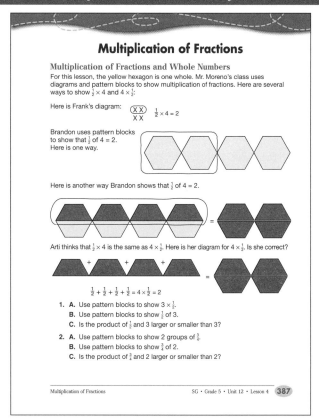

Student Guide - page 387

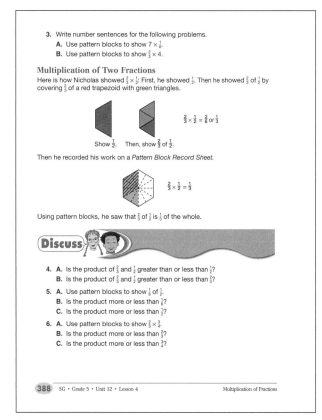

Student Guide - page 388

Student Guide (pp. 387–388)

Multiplication of Fractions

1.* **A–B.** See Figure 13 in Lesson Guide 4.

   C. The product of $\frac{1}{2}$ and 3 is less than 3 since we are finding a part of 3.

2.* **A–B.** See Figure 14 in Lesson Guide 4.

   C. The product of $\frac{3}{4}$ and 2 is smaller than 2 since we are finding a part of 2.

3. **A.**

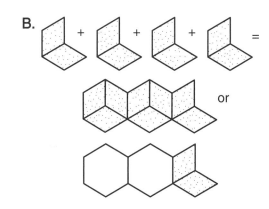

   $$\frac{1}{6} + \frac{1}{6} + \frac{1}{6} + \frac{1}{6} + \frac{1}{6} + \frac{1}{6} + \frac{1}{6} = 7 \times \frac{1}{6} = \frac{7}{6} \text{ or } 1\frac{1}{6}$$

   B.

   $$\frac{2}{3} + \frac{2}{3} + \frac{2}{3} + \frac{2}{3} = \frac{2}{3} \times 4 = \frac{8}{3} \text{ or } 2\frac{2}{3}$$

4.* **A.** Less than $\frac{1}{2}$

   B. Less than $\frac{2}{3}$

5.* **A.** See Figure 16 in Lesson Guide 4.

   B. Less than $\frac{1}{6}$

   C. Less than $\frac{1}{2}$

6. **A.** See Figure 17 in Lesson Guide 4.*

   B. Less than $\frac{2}{3}$

   C. Less than $\frac{3}{4}$

*Answers and/or discussion are included in the Lesson Guide.

Student Guide (p. 389)

7.* A. We can estimate the answer to be larger than $\frac{1}{12}$. See Figure 18 in Lesson Guide 4.

B. We can estimate the answer to be less than $\frac{1}{4}$. See Figure 18 in Lesson Guide 4.

C. We can estimate the answer to be less than $\frac{1}{2}$. See Figure 18 in Lesson Guide 4.

D. We can estimate the answer to be greater than 1 and less than 8. See Figure 18 in Lesson Guide 4.

Homework

1. We can estimate the answer to be more than $\frac{1}{4}$.

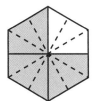

$$3 \times \tfrac{1}{4} = \tfrac{3}{4}$$

2. We can estimate the answer to be more than 1.

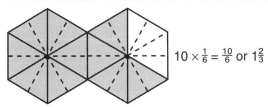

$$10 \times \tfrac{1}{6} = \tfrac{10}{6} \text{ or } 1\tfrac{2}{3}$$

3. We can estimate the answer to be greater than $\frac{1}{12}$.

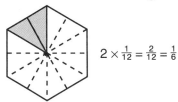

$$2 \times \tfrac{1}{12} = \tfrac{2}{12} = \tfrac{1}{6}$$

4. We can estimate the answer to be more than $\frac{1}{12}$.

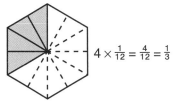

$$4 \times \tfrac{1}{12} = \tfrac{4}{12} = \tfrac{1}{3}$$

5. We can estimate the answer to be more than $\frac{1}{12}$ and less than 2.

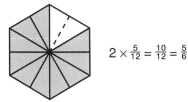

$$2 \times \tfrac{5}{12} = \tfrac{10}{12} = \tfrac{5}{6}$$

---

7. Use pattern blocks to show each of the following products.
- First, estimate the size of the product.
- Solve the problem and write a number sentence.
- Reduce fractions to lowest terms, but do not change improper fractions to mixed numbers.
- Record your work on a *Pattern Block Record Sheet*.

A. $3 \times \tfrac{1}{12}$ **B.** $\tfrac{1}{3} \times \tfrac{1}{4}$ **C.** $\tfrac{5}{6} \times \tfrac{1}{2}$ **D.** $8 \times \tfrac{1}{6}$

Homework

Use the *Pattern Block Record Sheet* Activity Pages to show each of the following products.

- First, estimate the size of the product.
- Solve the problem and write a number sentence.
- Reduce answers to lowest terms, but do not change improper fractions to mixed numbers.
- Record your work on a *Pattern Block Record Sheet*.

Follow the example: $6 \times \tfrac{1}{4}$

$$6 \times \tfrac{1}{4} = \tfrac{6}{4} = \tfrac{3}{2}$$

1. $3 \times \tfrac{1}{4} =$ **2.** $10 \times \tfrac{1}{6} =$

3. $2 \times \tfrac{1}{12} =$ **4.** $4 \times \tfrac{1}{12} =$

5. $2 \times \tfrac{5}{12} =$ **6.** $\tfrac{1}{2} \times \tfrac{1}{2} =$

7. $\tfrac{1}{3} \times \tfrac{3}{4} =$ **8.** $\tfrac{2}{3} \times \tfrac{1}{4} =$

9. $\tfrac{1}{2} \times \tfrac{1}{3} =$

Student Guide - page 389

---

*Answers and/or discussion are included in the Lesson Guide.

6. We can estimate the answer to be less than $\frac{1}{2}$.

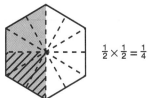

$\frac{1}{2} \times \frac{1}{2} = \frac{1}{4}$

7. We can estimate the answer to be less than $\frac{1}{3}$.

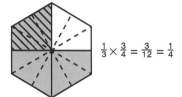

$\frac{1}{3} \times \frac{3}{4} = \frac{3}{12} = \frac{1}{4}$

8. We can estimate the answer to be less than $\frac{1}{4}$.

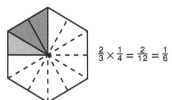

$\frac{2}{3} \times \frac{1}{4} = \frac{2}{12} = \frac{1}{6}$

9. We can estimate the answer to be less than $\frac{1}{3}$.

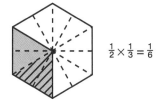

$\frac{1}{2} \times \frac{1}{3} = \frac{1}{6}$

Using Patterns to Multiply Fractions

Estimated Class Sessions

1

Lesson Overview

Part 1 of this lesson is a teacher-led activity. Students use paper folding to find the product of two fractions. They record their results and look for patterns to help them generalize a procedure for multiplying fractions.

In Part 2, *Student Guide* pages review the paper-folding activity. Students practice multiplying fractions with paper and pencil. They also discuss strategies for estimating products of fractions so they can decide if their answers are reasonable.

Key Content

- Multiplying fractions using paper folding.
- Multiplying fractions using paper and pencil.
- Estimating products of fractions.
- Solving problems in more than one way.

Math Facts

DPP Bit I reviews math facts in number sentences with variables.

Homework

1. Assign the Homework section in the *Student Guide.*
2. Assign Parts 3 and 4 of the Home Practice.
3. Use some or all of the *Party Problems* in Lesson 7 for homework.

Assessment

1. Use **Questions 10–14** in the Homework section as an assessment.
2. Use the *Observational Assessment Record* to note students' abilities to multiply fractions.
3. Transfer your observations to students' *Individual Assessment Record Sheets.*

Materials List

Supplies and Copies

Student	Teacher
Supplies for Each Student • several $8\frac{1}{2}$-by-11 inch sheets of scrap paper • crayons or colored pencils	**Supplies**
Copies	**Copies/Transparencies**

All blackline masters including assessment, transparency, and DPP masters are also on the Teacher Resource CD.

Student Books
Using Patterns to Multiply Fractions (*Student Guide* Pages 390–391)

Daily Practice and Problems and Home Practice
DPP items I–J (*Unit Resource Guide* Pages 17–18)
Home Practice Parts 3–4 (*Discovery Assignment Book* Page 190)

Note: Classrooms whose pacing differs significantly from the suggested pacing of the units should use the Math Facts Calendar in Section 4 of the *Facts Resource Guide* to ensure students receive the complete math facts program.

Assessment Tools
Observational Assessment Record (*Unit Resource Guide* Pages 11–12)
Individual Assessment Record Sheet (*Teacher Implementation Guide,* Assessment section)

Daily Practice and Problems

Suggestions for using the DPPs are on page 67.

I. Bit: More Division Fact Practice
(URG p. 17)

Find the number n that makes each sentence true.

A. $56 \div n = 8$

B. $480 \div n = 60$

C. $n \times 400 = 24{,}000$

D. $80 \times n = 3200$

E. $60 \times n = 420$

F. $n \div 7 = 400$

J. Task: Granola Bars (URG p. 18)

Lin's favorite granola bars come in packages of 10.

How many bars are in:

A. $\frac{1}{2}$ of a package?

B. $\frac{1}{10}$ of a package?

C. $\frac{3}{10}$ of a package?

D. $\frac{1}{5}$ of a package?

E. $\frac{3}{5}$ of a package?

F. $1\frac{1}{2}$ packages?

Part 1 Using Paper Folding to Multiply Fractions

To begin this activity, briefly review the homework from the previous lesson. Discuss **Question 9** ($\frac{1}{2} \times \frac{1}{3}$). Compare the results from using the *Pattern Block Record Sheet* in the homework to the results from using paper folding in this lesson.

In this part of the activity, students use paper folding to find the following products:

$$\frac{1}{2} \times \frac{1}{3}$$

$$\frac{3}{4} \times \frac{1}{2}$$

$$\frac{1}{2} \times \frac{3}{8}$$

$$\frac{5}{8} \times \frac{2}{3}$$

$$\frac{3}{4} \times \frac{2}{3}$$

After students find the answers, they will write complete number sentences for each problem. They will look for patterns in the number sentences to help them generalize a procedure for multiplying fractions. To be able to see the patterns, do **not** reduce the answers to lowest terms during this part of the lesson.

Before students read the *Student Guide* pages for this lesson, show them how to find the product of two fractions using paper folding as shown in Figure 19. To multiply $\frac{1}{2} \times \frac{1}{3}$, follow these steps:

- *Fold a scrap sheet of paper in thirds lengthwise.*
- *Unfold the paper, trace the folds, and color $\frac{1}{3}$ using one color crayon.*
- *Fold the paper in half horizontally.*
- *Unfold the paper, trace the fold, and use a different color to color $\frac{1}{2}$ of the $\frac{1}{3}$ section.*
- *The fraction colored with both colors is $\frac{1}{2}$ of $\frac{1}{3}$.*

When students complete the paper folding, ask:

- *How many parts is the paper divided into?* (6)
- *How many parts are shaded with both colors?* (1)
- *What fraction of the whole sheet of paper is $\frac{1}{2}$ of $\frac{1}{3}$?* ($\frac{1}{6}$)
- *Write a number sentence on your paper that shows the product of $\frac{1}{2}$ and $\frac{1}{3}$.* ($\frac{1}{2} \times \frac{1}{3} = \frac{1}{6}$. Write the number sentence on the board.)
- *Is $\frac{1}{2}$ of $\frac{1}{3}$ more or less than $\frac{1}{3}$? Why?* (Less. Because you are finding a part of $\frac{1}{3}$.)

Figure 19: *Using paper folding to find the product of $\frac{1}{2} \times \frac{1}{3}$*

$$\frac{1}{2} \times \frac{1}{3} = \frac{1}{6}$$

TIMS Tip

Remind students to crease each fold of paper well. This will make it easier to outline the parts when they unfold the paper.

Continue the lesson by using paper folding to find $\frac{3}{4}$ of $\frac{1}{2}$. See Figure 20. Students begin by folding a scrap sheet of paper in half lengthwise, unfolding the paper, tracing the fold, then coloring $\frac{1}{2}$. They fold the paper into fourths horizontally by folding the paper in half, then in half again. They then trace the folds and color $\frac{3}{4}$ of the colored section with a different color. Ask questions about this problem similar to the five questions above. Write $\frac{3}{4} \times \frac{1}{2} = \frac{3}{8}$ on the board under the first number sentence. It is important to encourage students to ask themselves if the answer is reasonable. They should see that the answer should be less than $\frac{1}{2}$ since multiplying by $\frac{3}{4}$ is finding a part of $\frac{1}{2}$.

Use a similar process to find $\frac{1}{2} \times \frac{3}{8}$, and $\frac{5}{8} \times \frac{2}{3}$, writing the results on the board in number sentences and discussing the number of parts in the whole and the number of parts shaded with two colors. Since $\frac{5}{8} \times \frac{2}{3}$ may be difficult for students, sample directions are given below. See Figure 21:

- *Fold a scrap sheet of paper into thirds lengthwise.*
- *Unfold the paper, trace the folds, and color $\frac{2}{3}$.*
- *Fold the paper into eighths horizontally by folding it in half (2 parts), then in half again (4 parts), and then in half one more time (8 parts).*
- *Unfold the paper, trace the folds, and color $\frac{5}{8}$ of the $\frac{2}{3}$ section using a different color.*
- *Count the total number of parts shown on the paper and count the number of parts that were colored twice.*
- *Write a number sentence for the product of $\frac{5}{8}$ and $\frac{2}{3}$. Do not reduce the answer to lowest terms. $\left(\frac{5}{8} \times \frac{2}{3} = \frac{10}{24}\right)$*

Finally, find $\frac{3}{4} \times \frac{2}{3}$ in the same way and write the results in a number sentence without reducing the answer to lowest terms. After the class finds all the products, ask them to look for patterns in the five number sentences:

$$\frac{1}{2} \times \frac{1}{3} = \frac{1}{6}$$
$$\frac{3}{4} \times \frac{1}{2} = \frac{3}{8}$$
$$\frac{1}{2} \times \frac{3}{8} = \frac{3}{16}$$
$$\frac{5}{8} \times \frac{2}{3} = \frac{10}{24}$$
$$\frac{3}{4} \times \frac{2}{3} = \frac{6}{12}$$

Students may see that to multiply fractions, we can multiply numerators and denominators as shown here:

$$\frac{3}{4} \times \frac{2}{3} = \frac{3 \times 2}{4 \times 3} = \frac{6}{12}$$

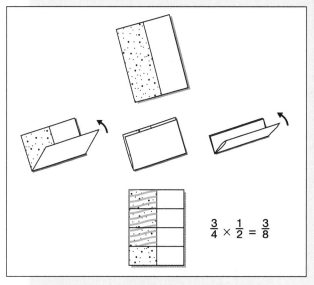

Figure 20: *Using paper folding to find the product of $\frac{3}{4} \times \frac{1}{2}$*

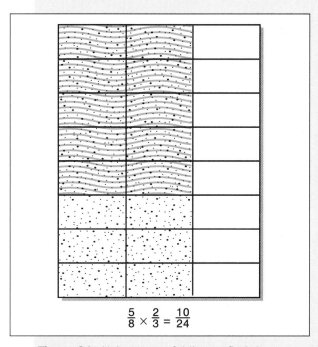

Figure 21: *Using paper folding to find the product of $\frac{5}{8} \times \frac{2}{3}$*

Using Patterns to Multiply Fractions

Mr. Moreno's class used paper folding to investigate multiplication of fractions. After solving several problems this way, they looked for a pattern to help them multiply fractions with pencil and paper. Shannon explained her group's strategy, using $\frac{3}{4} \times \frac{2}{3}$ as an example:

"To multiply $\frac{3}{4} \times \frac{2}{3}$, we folded a sheet of paper into thirds the long way, traced the folds, and colored $\frac{2}{3}$ yellow.

$\frac{2}{3}$

"Then we folded the paper into fourths the other way, traced the folds, and colored $\frac{3}{4}$ of the $\frac{2}{3}$ with blue.

"We saw that we had divided the paper into 4 × 3, or 12 parts. We colored 3 × 2, or 6 of the 12 parts blue. So, $\frac{6}{12}$ of the parts are colored blue. That's the same as $\frac{1}{2}$, so we wrote:

$\frac{3}{4} \times \frac{2}{3}$ of $\frac{2}{3}$

$$\frac{3}{4} \times \frac{2}{3} = \frac{3 \times 2}{4 \times 3} = \frac{6}{12} = \frac{1}{2}$$

"Our answer makes sense because we know that the answer should be less than $\frac{2}{3}$, since we were finding a part of $\frac{2}{3}$."

Discuss

1. A. Multiply $\frac{2}{3} \times \frac{3}{4}$ using paper and pencil. Reduce your answer to lowest terms.
    B. Is your answer reasonable? Why?
2. Felicia and Edward solved the problem $\frac{1}{2} \times \frac{4}{5}$ in two different ways. Felicia used paper and pencil and wrote the following:
    $$\frac{1}{2} \times \frac{4}{5} = \frac{1 \times 4}{2 \times 5} = \frac{4}{10}$$
    Edward reasoned that since $\frac{1}{2}$ of 4 is 2, then $\frac{1}{2}$ of $\frac{4}{5} = \frac{2}{5}$. Who is correct? Explain.

390 SG • Grade 5 • Unit 12 • Lesson 5   Using Patterns to Multiply Fractions

Student Guide - page 390 *(Answers on p. 69)*

3. Multiply $\frac{2}{3} \times 2$. (*Hint:* You can write 2 as $\frac{2}{1}$.)
    A. Should the answer be more or less than 2?
    B. Should the answer be more or less than 1?
    C. Solve the problem another way. Explain your strategy.
4. Solve. Reduce your answers to lowest terms. Is your answer reasonable?
    A. $\frac{2}{3} \times \frac{3}{5} =$ B. $\frac{1}{3} \times \frac{3}{10} =$ C. $\frac{3}{4} \times 6 =$ D. $\frac{2}{5} \times \frac{5}{8} =$

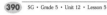
Homework

Find the following products. Write your answers in lowest terms.

1. $\frac{5}{8} \times \frac{1}{2} =$ 2. $\frac{1}{3} \times \frac{3}{4} =$ 3. $\frac{3}{10} \times \frac{1}{2} =$

4. $\frac{3}{5} \times \frac{3}{4} =$ 5. $\frac{3}{8} \times 4 =$ 6. $\frac{2}{3} \times \frac{2}{3} =$

7. $3 \times \frac{5}{6} =$ 8. $\frac{7}{10} \times \frac{1}{2} =$ 9. $10 \times \frac{4}{5} =$

10. $\frac{4}{5} \times \frac{3}{4} =$ 11. $8 \times \frac{2}{3} =$ 12. $\frac{2}{3} \times \frac{7}{8} =$

13. Brandon made a cheese pizza. He put pepperoni on $\frac{1}{2}$ of the pizza. He put onions on $\frac{3}{4}$ of the half with pepperoni. Draw a picture showing the toppings on the pizza.
    A. How much of the whole pizza has pepperoni and onions?
    B. How much of the whole pizza has only cheese?
    C. How much of the whole pizza has only pepperoni, but no onions?

14. A. Frank's guests ate $\frac{2}{3}$ of a cake at his party. How much cake was left over?
    B. The next day Frank ate $\frac{1}{4}$ of the leftover cake. How much of the whole cake did he eat the day after the party?

Using Patterns to Multiply Fractions   SG • Grade 5 • Unit 12 • Lesson 5 **391**

Student Guide - page 391 *(Answers on p. 69)*

Part 2 **Using Patterns to Multiply Fractions Using Paper and Pencil**

The solution and strategy for solving $\frac{3}{4} \times \frac{2}{3}$ is discussed in detail in the *Using Patterns to Multiply Fractions* Activity Pages in the *Student Guide.* On those pages, a student explains that to show the multiplication, the paper is divided into 4 × 3 or 12 parts; 3 × 2 or 6 of those parts are colored twice. The discussion connects the paper folding with a paper-and-pencil procedure for multiplying fractions. As you begin work with paper-and-pencil procedures, remind students to check for the reasonableness of their answers.

Question 1A asks students to use the pattern to find the product of $\frac{2}{5}$ and $\frac{3}{4}$ and to reduce the answer to lowest terms. In *Question 1B,* they must decide if the answer is reasonable. The product $\frac{3}{10}$ is a reasonable answer since it is less than $\frac{3}{4}$. Finding a part of $\frac{3}{4}$ should result in a fraction smaller than $\frac{3}{4}$.

Question 2 challenges students to think about multiplication of fractions in more than one way. Two students solve the same problem. One uses standard paper-and-pencil procedures, and the other uses reasoning to solve the problem. Both methods produce a correct answer, although the first student did not give the answer in lowest terms.

Question 3 extends the pattern to the multiplication of a fraction and a whole number ($\frac{3}{5} \times 2$). Students are reminded that 2 can be written as $\frac{2}{1}$, so $\frac{3}{5} \times 2 = \frac{3}{5} \times \frac{2}{1} = \frac{3 \times 2}{5 \times 1} = \frac{6}{5}$.

Question 3C asks students to solve the problem another way. For example, $\frac{3}{5} \times 2$ can also be written as $\frac{3}{5} + \frac{3}{5} = \frac{6}{5}$.

Question 4 provides some practice before students are asked to solve similar problems on their own. As the class discusses the solutions to the problems, encourage them to discuss strategies for determining the reasonableness of their answers. Also, through class discussion of student strategies, encourage students to think about other possible ways of solving the problems besides using the standard pencil-and-paper procedure. For example, for *Question 4B,* students may reason that since $\frac{1}{3}$ of 3 is 1, $\frac{1}{3}$ of $\frac{3}{10}$ is $\frac{1}{10}$.

Journal Prompt

Find a way to solve $\frac{1}{4} \times \frac{4}{5}$ without multiplying the numerators and denominators. Describe your strategy.

Math Facts

DPP item I reviews math facts in number sentences with unknown dividends, divisors, and factors.

Homework and Practice

- Assign the Homework section in the *Student Guide.*
- Assign DPP item J that reviews multiplying a whole number by a fraction.
- Assign some or all of the *Party Problems* in Lesson 7 for homework.
- Assign Parts 3 and 4 of the Home Practice that review fractions, percents, and computation.

Answers for Parts 3 and 4 of the Home Practice are in the Answer Key at the end of this lesson and at the end of this unit.

Assessment

- Use *Questions 10–14* in the Homework section to assess students' abilities to multiply fractions.
- Use the *Observational Assessment Record* to note students' abilities to multiply fractions.
- Transfer your observations to students' *Individual Assessment Record Sheets.*

Name _____ Date _____

PART 3 Fractions

Solve the following problems. Estimate to see if your answers are reasonable.

1. A. $\frac{1}{3} \times 15 =$ B. $\frac{1}{8} \times 24 =$ C. $\frac{2}{3} \times \frac{1}{6} =$

    D. $\frac{1}{5} \times \frac{5}{8} =$ E. $\frac{1}{12} \times \frac{2}{5} =$ F. $\frac{3}{8} \times 16 =$

    G. $\frac{1}{4}$ of $2.00 =$ H. $\frac{2}{5}$ of $50 =$ I. $\frac{3}{4}$ of $24 =$

2. Solve Question 1D a different way. Explain your strategy.

PART 4 Analyze the Class

In a class of 24 students:

1. Of the students, 25% are left-handed. How many students are left-handed?

2. One-third of the class is wearing jeans. How many students are wearing jeans?

3. Extra credit math work was done by 18 students. What fraction of the class did extra credit work?

4. What percent of the class did extra credit work?

5. Twelve students are girls. What fraction of students are boys?

190 DAB • Grade 5 • Unit 12   USING FRACTIONS

Discovery Assignment Book **- page 190** *(Answers on p. 70)*

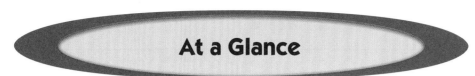

At a Glance

Math Facts and Daily Practice and Problems

DPP Bit I reviews math facts in number sentences with variables. Task J reviews multiplying whole numbers by fractions.

Part 1. Using Paper Folding to Multiply Fractions

1. Demonstrate to students how to find the product of $\frac{1}{2} \times \frac{1}{3}$ using paper folding.
2. Discuss the answer using the discussion prompts in the Lesson Guide. Then write a number sentence for the problem.
3. Repeat the procedure for four more multiplication problems: $\frac{3}{4} \times \frac{1}{2}$, $\frac{1}{2} \times \frac{3}{8}$, $\frac{5}{8} \times \frac{2}{3}$, and $\frac{3}{4} \times \frac{2}{3}$. Solve each problem using paper folding, discuss the problem including the reasonableness of the results, and write a number sentence.
4. Look for patterns in the multiplication sentences and use the patterns to generalize a procedure for multiplying fractions using paper and pencil.

Part 2. Using Patterns to Multiply Fractions Using Paper and Pencil

1. Read and discuss the example on the *Using Patterns to Multiply Fractions* Activity Pages in the *Student Guide*.
2. Discuss *Questions 1–4* in the *Student Guide*. Encourage students to look for more than one way to solve the problems and always to check that their answers are reasonable.

Homework

1. Assign the Homework section in the *Student Guide*.
2. Assign Parts 3 and 4 of the Home Practice.
3. Use some or all of the *Party Problems* in Lesson 7 for homework.

Assessment

1. Use *Questions 10–14* in the Homework section as an assessment.
2. Use the *Observational Assessment Record* to note students' abilities to multiply fractions.
3. Transfer your observations to students' *Individual Assessment Record Sheets*.

Answer Key is on pages 69–70.

Notes:

Student Guide (pp. 390–391)

Using Patterns to Multiply Fractions

1. **A.** $\frac{2}{5} \times \frac{3}{4} = \frac{2 \times 3}{5 \times 4} = \frac{6}{20} = \frac{3}{10}$

   B. Yes; the answer should be less than $\frac{3}{4}$, since we are finding a part of $\frac{3}{4}$.*

2. Both students are right. If Felicia reduces her answer to lowest terms, she gets $\frac{2}{5}$ which is the same answer Edward wrote.*

3. $\frac{6}{5}$ or $1\frac{1}{5}$*

   A. Less than 2, since we are finding a part of 2.

   B. More than 1. Since $\frac{3}{5}$ is greater than $\frac{1}{2}$, then $\frac{3}{5}$ of 2 should be more than $\frac{1}{2}$ of 2.

   C. $\frac{3}{5} \times 2 = \frac{3}{5} + \frac{3}{5} = \frac{6}{5}$*

4. **A.** $\frac{2}{5}$; the answer is reasonable since it should be less than $\frac{3}{5}$.

   B. $\frac{1}{10}$; the answer is reasonable since it should be less than $\frac{3}{10}$.*

   C. $\frac{9}{2}$ or $4\frac{1}{2}$; the answer is reasonable since it should be less than 6.

   D. $\frac{1}{4}$; the answer is reasonable since it should be less than $\frac{5}{8}$.

Homework

1. $\frac{5}{16}$

2. $\frac{1}{4}$

3. $\frac{3}{20}$

4. $\frac{9}{20}$

5. $\frac{3}{2}$ or $1\frac{1}{2}$

6. $\frac{4}{9}$

7. $\frac{5}{2}$ or $2\frac{1}{2}$

8. $\frac{7}{20}$

9. 8

10. $\frac{3}{5}$

11. $\frac{16}{3} = 5\frac{1}{3}$

12. $\frac{7}{12}$

13.

   A. $\frac{3}{8}$ **B.** $\frac{1}{2}$ **C.** $\frac{1}{8}$

14. **A.** $\frac{1}{3}$

   B. $\frac{1}{4} \times \frac{1}{3} = \frac{1}{12}$

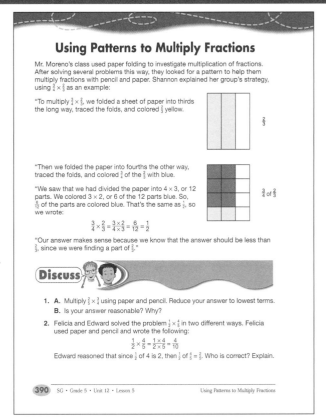

Student Guide - page 390

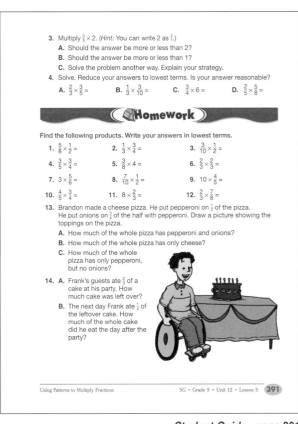

Student Guide - page 391

*Answers and/or discussion are included in the Lesson Guide.

Name _____ Date _____

PART 3 **Fractions**

Solve the following problems. Estimate to see if your answers are reasonable.

1. A. $\frac{1}{3} \times 15 =$ 　　B. $\frac{1}{8} \times 24 =$ 　　C. $\frac{2}{3} \times \frac{1}{6} =$

 D. $\frac{1}{5} \times \frac{5}{6} =$ 　　E. $\frac{1}{12} \times \frac{2}{5} =$ 　　F. $\frac{3}{8} \times 16 =$

 G. $\frac{1}{4}$ of $2.00 =$ 　　H. $\frac{2}{5}$ of $50 =$ 　　I. $\frac{3}{4}$ of $24 =$

2. Solve Question 1D a different way. Explain your strategy.

PART 4 **Analyze the Class**

In a class of 24 students:

1. Of the students, 25% are left-handed. How many students are left-handed?

2. One-third of the class is wearing jeans. How many students are wearing jeans?

3. Extra credit math work was done by 18 students. What fraction of the class did extra credit work?

4. What percent of the class did extra credit work?

5. Twelve students are girls. What fraction of students are boys?

Copyright © Kendall/Hunt Publishing Company

Discovery Assignment Book - page 190

Discovery Assignment Book (p. 190)

Home Practice*

Part 3. Fractions

1. A. 5 　　　　　　　　B. 3
 C. $\frac{1}{9}$ 　　　　　　　D. $\frac{1}{6}$
 E. $\frac{1}{30}$ 　　　　　　F. 6
 G. 50¢ 　　　　　　H. $20
 I. $18

2. Two possible strategies:
$\frac{1}{5} \times \frac{5}{6} = \frac{5}{30} = \frac{1}{6}$; $\frac{1}{5}$ of 5 is 1, so $\frac{1}{5}$ of $\frac{5}{6}$ is $\frac{1}{6}$.

Part 4. Analyze the Class

1. 6 　　　　　　　2. 8
3. $\frac{3}{4}$ 　　　　　　4. 75%
5. $\frac{1}{2}$

---

*Answers for all the Home Practice in the *Discovery Assignment Book* are at the end of the unit.

Lesson 6

Peanut Soup

Estimated Class Sessions

1

Lesson Overview

George Washington Carver shows his students at Tuskegee Institute the many food and nonfood products he has derived from peanut products in his lab. He tells them he promised to help local farmers find a market for their peanut crops, but that local businessmen do not yet accept the idea that peanuts will make a good investment.

Together, Carver and his students decide to demonstrate the versatility of peanuts in a dramatic way by inviting a group of businessmen to a luncheon of dishes containing peanuts. As they test the recipes and prepare the meal, Carver's students use fractions to convert recipes to the needed size. They also use various types of reasoning to create a schedule for cooking the meal.

In spite of minor setbacks, the meal is a great success, and the businessmen agree to support the farmers.

Key Content

- Creating a time schedule.
- Connecting mathematics to science and social studies: Learning about George Washington Carver.

Key Vocabulary

- economic potential
- goobers
- legumes
- nitrogen fixation
- ratio

Math Facts

DPP Bit K reviews math facts in division sentences with quotients as mixed numbers.

Homework

Assign Parts 5 and 6 of the Home Practice.

Curriculum Sequence

Before This Unit

In Unit 4 Lesson 7 students were introduced to George Washington Carver in the Adventure Book *George Washington Carver: A Man of Measure.*

After This Unit

The context of increasing or decreasing the number of servings made from a recipe will be used to review ratios and introduce proportions in Unit 13 Lesson 1.

Materials List

Supplies and Copies

Student	Teacher
Supplies for Each Student	**Supplies**
Copies	**Copies/Transparencies**

All blackline masters including assessment, transparency, and DPP masters are also on the Teacher Resource CD.

Student Books
Peanut Soup (*Adventure Book* Pages 77–92)

Daily Practice and Problems and Home Practice
DPP items K–L (*Unit Resource Guide* Page 18)
Home Practice Parts 5–6 (*Discovery Assignment Book* Page 191)

Note: Classrooms whose pacing differs significantly from the suggested pacing of the units should use the Math Facts Calendar in Section 4 of the *Facts Resource Guide* to ensure students receive the complete math facts program.

Daily Practice and Problems

Suggestions for using the DPPs are on page 79.

K. Bit: Division (URG p. 18)

Try to solve the following problems in your head. Write the quotients as mixed numbers. Fractions should be in lowest terms.

A. $30 \div 7 =$ B. $60 \div 8 =$

C. $47 \div 6 =$ D. $26 \div 6 =$

E. $51 \div 6 =$ F. $35 \div 4 =$

L. Task: Multiplying Fractions
(URG p. 18)

Multiply these fractions. Reduce answers to lowest terms. Estimate to see if your answers are reasonable.

A. $\frac{1}{2} \times \frac{1}{4} =$ B. $\frac{1}{4} \times \frac{1}{4} =$

C. $\frac{2}{3} \times \frac{1}{2} =$ D. $\frac{3}{8} \times \frac{1}{6} =$

E. $\frac{5}{8} \times \frac{2}{3} =$ F. $\frac{1}{2} \times \frac{3}{5} =$

Teaching the Activity

We suggest that students first read the *Adventure Book* to enjoy and understand the story. Then, use the following prompts to lead a class discussion.

Content Note

Tuskegee Normal and Industrial Institute was founded in 1881 by Booker T. Washington as a school where African-American boys and girls could learn to use science in practical ways. Its students were of diverse ages and economic backgrounds; some lived at the school, and some lived nearby. In addition to their studies, the students worked at the school, farming the gardens, tending the animals, helping in the kitchens, or constructing new buildings. Today Tuskegee Institute and the Carver Foundation continue research in the natural sciences. The Tuskegee Archives contain records of black history since 1896.

Adventure Book - page 79

Peanut Soup

Carver pointed to his lab table, which was covered with vials, pans, and bottles. "Everything you see here—this shoe polish, this face cream, even this glass of milk—I made from peanuts. The possibilities are endless! There's shaving cream, house paint—and look at this! I think this would make excellent linoleum! I made it from peanut shells."

"You made all this from *goobers*?" asked Eugene. "All this stuff?"

Before Carver could answer, young Buford, the smallest of the group, asked, "Why did you want to make stuff out of goobers?"

Carver gestured toward the window and the farmland beyond. "Well, Buford, it's because I made a promise to the farmers around here, and they've been asking me when I'm going to keep it."

"A promise?" Louis asked.

Adventure Book - page 79

"That's right," explained Carver. "I've been telling the farmers to plant peanuts instead of growing cotton. Our work here at Tuskegee has shown that peanuts are good for the soil and the crops they grow now are ruining the soil. You see, cotton takes nitrogen from the soil, and nitrogen must be present for most plants to grow. Peanuts and other legumes like cowpeas and soybeans put nitrogen back into the soil by 'fixing' it so that the plants can use it."

While Carver spoke, Eugene and Buford studied the items on the lab table. "Is there anything good to eat here?" Buford asked. "Sure, Buford," replied a skeptical Eugene, "Why don't you take a bite of that linoleum and tell me what you think!"

Alberta reminded Carver that he hadn't yet explained what his promise to the farmers had been.

"I promised that they would be able to make a profit by selling their peanuts," Carver said. "I told them that there would be a good market for their crops. Trouble is, I was the only one who could imagine the value of the peanut. But now, I have found dozens of ways for peanuts to be used!"

"Wow, Professor," exclaimed Louis, "I can hardly believe you made all of these things from goobers! Could I try the shoe polish?"

Adventure Book - page 80

Page 79

- *What was Professor Carver working on so hard in his lab?*

He had been developing products made from peanuts.

- *What kinds of products did Carver make from peanuts?*

Shoe polish, face cream, milk, shaving cream, linoleum, house paint

Page 80

- *What are legumes, and how do they affect the soil?*
- *What was Carver's promise to the farmers? What did he do to try to keep it?*

Carver promised the farmers that they could make a profit selling peanuts. He experimented and found many new uses for the peanut.

Content Note

Legumes are a family of plants including peas, beans, soybeans, peanuts, and clover. Legumes play a very important role in the process of farming. Nodules on the roots of legumes contain special bacteria capable of transforming unusable atmospheric nitrogen into a form of nitrogen that is usable by living organisms. This process is called **nitrogen fixation.**

Page 81

- *Why did Carver want the businessmen to know the many uses of the peanut?*

So they would buy the farmers' peanut crops and open factories to make peanut products.

- *What was Louis's idea?*

To have a big dinner of their favorite peanut dishes to impress the businessmen.

Peanut Soup

"Yes—try anything you like. And let me know what you think."

"This face cream is wonderful!" said Alberta. "Now will you show the farmers how to make all these things?"

"I'm afraid it's not that simple, Alberta," Carver replied. "Farmers don't have the time or the equipment to make all these things for themselves. What the farmers need is for someone to buy their peanuts. They need businessmen to open factories to make peanut products. Unfortunately, the businessmen around here don't think very highly of our lowly goober. I could show these products to local businessmen, and they would listen politely, but they would probably still think that goobers are only good for hog feed and fertilizer. I wish there were some way I could get them to 'catch the vision' and see all the economic potential that is locked up in a little peanut."

Buford had been waiting for a chance to be heard. "But, Professor, I don't see anything to eat here! The thing I like best about goobers is eating them. Why, all the folks I know like to eat goobers—doesn't everybody?"

Eugene was doubtful. "I don't think so, Buford—I know Black folks eat goobers, but I've never seen any white folks eating them."

"Hey, Professor—this is giving me an idea!" exclaimed Louis. "Maybe if we show those businessmen just how good goobers are to eat, they might be more willing to invest their money."

"You know, Louis, that's not a bad idea. What exactly did you have in mind?"

AB • Grade 5 • Unit 12 • Lesson 6   81

Adventure Book - page 81

Page 83

- *Why did Eugene get too much flour for Alberta?*

Because he followed a recipe exactly, without considering the number of people it would serve.

Peanut Soup

Alberta interrupted. "Please, just read the recipe and fetch the right amount of flour!"

Eugene picked up an enormous metal bowl and headed for the pantry. "If you say so."

Alberta addressed two of her fellow students, "While Eugene's getting the flour, we can look for the right-size pans."

Eugene returned from the pantry with a huge bowl of flour. "Here you go, Alberta. This is the first batch—I figure I'll have to fetch about ten more bowls to have enough."

Alberta stared down at him. "What are you thinking? There is enough flour here for two banquets!"

"No, ma'am," Eugene replied. "That recipe says plain as day that we need 70 pounds of flour for the bread."

Alberta took up the recipe. "Let me see that."

She read the instructions. "Well, no wonder! This recipe makes enough bread to feed half the students at Tuskegee! We'll have to make much less than this recipe says to make."

AB • Grade 5 • Unit 12 • Lesson 6   83

Adventure Book - page 83

Peanut Soup

"That's a good idea," joked Eugene. "Maybe if we cut it down far enough, those businessmen won't even notice the peanuts in it."

"Don't be silly, Eugene. The amount of peanuts—I mean the ratio—of peanuts to bread will stay the same."

"Ratio?" asked Eugene.

"Relax," replied Alberta. "A ratio is just a fraction. We can use fractions to solve our flour problem."

"How?"

"Let's follow the Professor's advice and start with what we know. Look at your bread recipe and tell me how many people it serves."

Eugene looked at the recipe. "This says, 'Feeds 240.'"

PEANUT BREAD INGREDIENTS

· FLOUR
· BLANCHED AND GROUND PEANUTS
· MILK
· BAKING POWDER
· SALT

"But we'll only have 12 men at the luncheon," Alberta pointed out.

"Yeah—so the recipe you gave me is way too big."

"Right! So can you tell me how much flour you'll need for our bread?"

"Let's see . . ." Eugene thought. "I think I can. If we divide 240 people by 12 people, we get 20. This means the recipe makes 20 times more than we need. So we should divide each ingredient by 20."

"Good thinking, Eugene! You're right. You do know how to use ratios!"

Eugene was puzzled. "Ratios? When did I use a ratio?"

Alberta patiently wrote out the ratio she had in mind:

$$\frac{\text{people served at luncheon}}{\text{people served with recipe}} = \frac{12 \text{ people}}{240 \text{ people}}$$

Eugene easily saw what Alberta was trying to say. "So ratios are like fractions," he said. "But wait a minute! That's not the way I did it. I divided 240 by 12. What you have is just the opposite. You are dividing 12 by 240. In arithmetic we learned that we always divide the numerator by the denominator."

Adventure Book - page 84

Discussion Prompts

Page 84

* *What is a ratio? Give an example from the story.*

A **ratio** is a comparison of quantities, often expressed as a fraction. The ratio involved here is the number of people served at the luncheon compared with the number of people served by Alberta's recipe ($\frac{12 \text{ people}}{240 \text{ people}}$).

Peanut Soup

"Go ahead and divide and see what you get," suggested Alberta.

Eugene scribbled on the paper and announced, "I get .05 for an answer."

"Good," said Alberta. "Can you write that as a fraction?"

"Sure," answered Eugene. ".05 = $\frac{5}{100}$, and if I reduce that I get $\frac{1}{20}$."

Alberta pounced upon his answer: "That's why you divided the flour by 20! You were calculating the amount you will need for $\frac{1}{20}$ of the original recipe."

"I get it!" Eugene wrote the following equation on the paper: $\frac{12}{240} = .05 = \frac{5}{100} = \frac{1}{20}$. "These are all different ways of saying the same thing."

"So," said Alberta. "We agree that we need to find one-twentieth of all these ingredients. First, take the flour. What's $\frac{1}{20}$ of 70 pounds?"

"Let's write it down," suggested Eugene, "so we can figure it out."

Alberta and Eugene sat down with a pencil and paper. "Seventy pounds divided by twenty is three and one-half pounds," Alberta said, "so we need three and one-half pounds of flour for the smaller recipe." She wrote: 70 pounds ÷ 20 = $3\frac{1}{2}$ pounds.

Adventure Book - page 85

Page 85

* *How would you find $\frac{1}{20}$ of 70 pounds of flour?*

Answers will vary.

Page 86

- *If there are about 4 cups of flour in a pound, how many cups do you need for $3\frac{1}{2}$ pounds? How would you solve this problem?*

The answer is 14 cups. Solutions will vary. Alberta changed $3\frac{1}{2}$ pounds to $\frac{7}{2}$ pounds and then multiplied $\frac{7}{2}$ by 4. Another strategy is to multiply $4 \times 3\frac{1}{2}$ by multiplying $4 \times 3 = 12$ and $4 \times \frac{1}{2} = 2$. Then $12 + 2 = 14$ cups.

- *How many tablespoons are in a quarter-cup (one-fourth cup)?*

4 tablespoons

- *How many times will Josephine have to refill the quarter-cup to measure 12 tablespoons?*

Three times. She needs $\frac{3}{4}$ cup of flour.

Peanut Soup

"Should I go to the lab and find a scale to weigh the flour?" Eugene asked.

"There's no need—we can easily measure it in cups," Alberta said. "There are about four cups of flour in a pound, and we need three and one-half pounds, so how many cups is that?"

"Well, let me see . . . three and one-half is seven halves, and seven halves times four equals 28 halves, which equals . . .14! We need 14 cups of flour."

Alberta wrote: 4 cups $\times$ $3\frac{1}{2}$ = 14 cups.

"Good," Alberta said. "Now let's figure out the rest of the ingredients."

Meanwhile, Carver checked up on Josephine. "How's the soup recipe coming?" he asked.

"Fine!" Josephine replied. "The recipe only makes enough for four people, but since we're cooking for 12, we have to triple everything. We're just measuring the flour now. I figure we need 12 tablespoons. Charles, hand me that tablespoon, will you?"

Carver raised his hand. "Hold on a minute, Josephine—it will take a long time to measure 12 tablespoons one at a time. Can you think of a faster way?"

"Well, we have larger measures, but I don't know how many tablespoons they hold," Josephine said.

"That should be easy to figure out," Carver answered. "Why don't you find out how many tablespoons it takes to fill this quarter-cup?"

"The quarter-cup holds exactly four tablespoons," Josephine said. "Now I can use it to measure the flour."

"Very good, Josephine. I'll check back again in a while to see how you're doing."

86   AB · Grade 5 · Unit 12 · Lesson 6

Adventure Book - page 86

Page 88

- *How did Louis decide to start making the cookies at a quarter till twelve?*

He allowed 15 min (to mix and shape the cookies) + 45 min (to bake 3 trays at 15 min per tray) = 60 min or 1 hr.

Louis added an extra 15 min "to be on the safe side," so they needed to start baking cookies 1 hr and 15 min before the luncheon or at 11:45.

Peanut Soup

Louis added, "We also have to figure out whether to bake all the cookies at the same time or whether we'll need to do them in different batches."

"Good thinking," agreed Carver. "I have to use the oven for the mock chicken starting at noon, so we can only bake one tray of cookies at a time."

Buford figured out loud. "So if we make 3 cookies each for 12 people, that's 36 cookies, or three dozen. We can put a dozen cookies on a tray. That means we'll need three trays."

Louis was impressed. "Hey, that's really using your head, Buford! So I'll have to bake three trays of cookies, one tray at a time. If we allow 15 minutes to mix and shape the cookies and add an extra 15 minutes to be on the safe side, we should start the cookies at a quarter till twelve."

Louis was pleased with their planning. "Finally we have a schedule!"

> *11:45 Start making cookies.*
> *12:00 Put mock chicken loaf in oven.*
> *12:00 Begin creamed vegetable.*

"This meal is shaping up very nicely," Carver declared. "I can't wait until Saturday to see the expressions on the faces of our guests when I tell them what they've been eating!"

"Well, I can wait!" Eugene said. "In fact, I think I'll just go wait in my room. Just let me know when it's all over."

88   AB · Grade 5 · Unit 12 · Lesson 6

Adventure Book - page 88

Buford was quick to apologize for the trouble. "I sure am sorry, Professor—I was only trying to help. I'll do better now! I'll find the best greens, and I'll carry them for you, and I'll help you wash them and toss them—these will be the best darned greens those old high-hats ever ate! These greens—"

"Buford," interrupted Carver, stooping to pick some greens, "there's no need to be disrespectful toward our guests. Some of these 'high-hats,' as you call them, are good friends of mine, and many of them have done a lot to help Tuskegee."

"Yes, sir. I'm sorry. Hey, Professor—look at all these dandelion greens! There are enough here for ten luncheons."

"Yes, but wild greens taste best when you use a variety. I'd like to find some pokeweed and some rabbit tobacco. Let's look over there . . ."

Meanwhile, the students were getting nervous in the kitchen. "I hope Professor Carver returns soon," said Eugene as he looked out the window. "I don't see him anywhere. Those greens might be the only good part of this meal!"

Alberta looked around the kitchen. "Everything's ready! All we need are the greens. But where can Professor Carver be?"

AB • Grade 5 • Unit 12 • Lesson 6   **91**

Adventure Book - page 91

Page 91

- *Why did Carver want to have greens with the meal? Why did he want several different kinds?*

According to the story, a mix of greens tastes better than a single type by itself. Also, the greens provide nutritional balance.

Historical Note

George Washington Carver wrote bulletins about the medicinal and nutritional properties of wild plants and vegetables. During the first World War, his bulletins helped people locate, harvest, and prepare wild greens that were not only good to eat, but also good for them. One such green was the pokeweed as shown here.

Peanut Soup

Eugene looked out the door. "I don't know. Maybe they decided to skip this nutty lunch!"

Just then, Carver and Buford returned with their arms full of greens. "Here we are! How's it going?"

"Thank goodness you're back!" Alberta cried. "You're just in time to greet the guests!"

Buford turned to Eugene. "Quick—help me wash these greens!"

The Tuskegee luncheon was a great success. After the meal, when the guests had eaten enthusiastically and praised the cooks, Carver announced that every dish had contained peanuts.

The businessmen were amazed and asked many questions. They learned that milk and butter—even pickles—could be made from the lowly goober, as well as cheese, coffee, and many useful nonfood products. Carver explained how the peanut was an easy crop to grow and how it enriched the soil. The businessmen agreed that there might be a profitable future for the peanut.

And Eugene scrubbed all the pots.

92   AB • Grade 5 • Unit 12 • Lesson 6

Adventure Book- page 92

Page 92

- *Were the guests surprised to learn that all the dishes contained peanuts? Was the luncheon a success?*

Yes. The businessmen enjoyed all the dishes and were amazed to find that there were peanuts in all of them. They agreed that peanuts might be profitable.

Content Note

Peanut Soup is based on more than one true incident in Carver's career in Tuskegee. To stage dramatic presentations of his work with the peanut, sweet potato, or cowpea, Carver delighted in serving meals made entirely with dishes containing these items. He waited until after the guests had finished their meal to tell them what they had eaten. He invariably took the opportunity to demonstrate other nonfood uses of the legume and won over many skeptics in this way.

Math Facts

DPP Bit K reviews math facts in division sentences with quotients as mixed numbers.

Homework and Practice

- Assign DPP Task L for practice multiplying fractions.
- Assign Parts 5 and 6 of the Home Practice that review operations with fractions and decimals and coordinate geometry.

Answers for Parts 5 and 6 of the Home Practice are in the Answer Key at the end of this lesson and at the end of this unit.

Extension

- Ask students to take a favorite family recipe and expand it to serve 12 people.
- Students can make a menu for a special meal with their family and make a list of ingredients they will need and plan a schedule for preparing the meal.

Literature Connections

- Adair, Gene. *George Washington Carver: Botanist.* Chelsea House Publishers, New York, 1989.
- Carter, Andy, and Carol Saller. *George Washington Carver.* Carolrhoda Books, Inc., Minneapolis, MN, 2001.
- Mitchel, Barbara. *A Pocketful of Goobers.* Carolrhoda Books, Inc., Minneapolis, MN, 1989.
- Moore, Eva. *The Story of George Washington Carver.* Scholastic, New York, 1995.

Resources

- Carver, George W. "How to Grow the Peanut and 105 Ways of Preparing it for Human Consumption." *Bulletin No. 31.* Experiment Station, Tuskegee Normal and Industrial Institute, Tuskegee, AL, June 1925.
- Carver, George W. "Nature's Garden for Victory and Peace." *Bulletin No. 43.* Experiment Station, Tuskegee Normal and Industrial Institute, Tuskegee, AL, March 1942.
- Holt, Rackham. *George Washington Carver: An American Biography.* Doubleday, New York, 1961.
- Kremer, Gary R. *George Washington Carver: In His Own Words.* University of Missouri Press, Columbia, MO, 1987.
- McMurry, Linda L. *George Washington Carver: Scientist and Symbol.* Oxford University Press, New York, 1981.

Name _____ Date _____

PART 5 Let's Practice

Use paper and pencil to solve the following. Use a separate sheet of paper to show your work.

A. $3\frac{4}{5} + 7\frac{1}{4} =$ B. $862 \times 9 =$ C. $94 \times 34 =$

D. $53.68 + 0.432 =$ E. $7341 \div 9 =$ F. $82 - 14.65 =$

PART 6 Working with Coordinates

I. A. Plot the coordinates in the table. Record the ordered pairs. Label the points with a letter on the graph.

Point	x-coordinate	y-coordinate	Ordered Pairs
A	-2	-1	
B	-3	-3	
C	-1	-3	
D	1	3	

B. You will need a ruler for this problem. If 1 cm = 200 cm on the graph, what is the distance between A and D?

USING FRACTIONS   DAB • Grade 5 • Unit 12 **191**

Discovery Assignment Book - page 191 (Answers on p. 80)

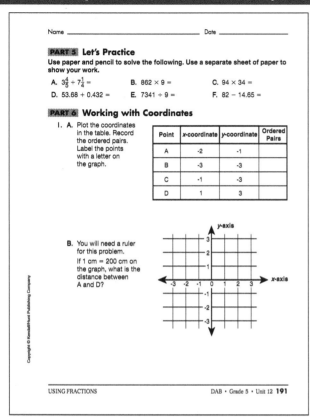

Discovery Assignment Book - page 191

Discovery Assignment Book (p. 191)

Home Practice*

Part 5. Let's Practice

A. $11\frac{1}{20}$ **B.** 7758

C. 3196   **D.** 54.112

E. 815 R6 or $815\frac{2}{3}$ **F.** 67.35

Part 6. Working with Coordinates

I. A.

Point	x-coordinate	y-coordinate	Ordered Pair
A	-2	-1	(-2, -1)
B	-3	-3	(-3, -3)
C	-1	-3	(-1, -3)
D	1	3	(1, 3)

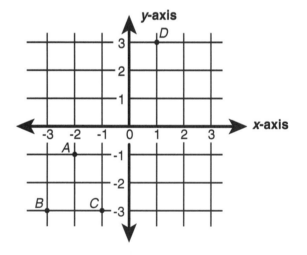

B. 1000 cm

*Answers for all the Home Practice in the *Discovery Assignment Book* are at the end of the unit.

80   URG • Grade 5 • Unit 12 • Lesson 6 • Answer Key

Party Problems

Lesson Overview

Students solve a variety of multistep word problems.

Key Content

- Solving multistep word problems.
- Solving problems involving fractions.
- Communicating solutions orally and in writing.
- Choosing appropriate methods and tools to calculate (calculators, paper and pencil, or mental math).
- Choosing to find an estimate or an exact answer.

Homework

Assign some or all of the problems for homework.

Materials List

Supplies and Copies

Student	Teacher
Supplies for Each Student • calculator	**Supplies**
Copies	**Copies/Transparencies** .

All blackline masters including assessment, transparency, and DPP masters are also on the Teacher Resource CD.

Student Books

Party Problems (*Student Guide* Pages 392–393)

Teaching the Activity

This problem set can serve many purposes. It can present opportunities for students to choose appropriate methods to solve problems. You can also use it to supplement homework for the unit or as an assessment.

Questions 1–6 cover concepts learned in this unit. *Questions 7–10* review concepts learned in previous units. You may choose to assign some or all of the problems to reinforce concepts in preparation for the midterm test in Lesson 8.

Homework and Practice

Assign some or all of the questions for homework.

Party Problems

Solve the following problems. Show how you solved each problem.

1. Jeff's sister made a HAPPY BIRTHDAY sign for Jeff. Since Jeff is 10 years old, his sister drew 10 flowers. She colored $\frac{2}{5}$ of the flowers yellow and the rest she colored red. What fraction of the flowers are red?

2. At the beginning of the party, Jeff set 18 cups of lemonade on the table. After the party was over, $\frac{1}{6}$ of the cups of lemonade were left. How many cups of lemonade did Jeff's guests drink?

3. Jeff's mother bought 2 bags of balloons. Each bag contained 8 balloons. She used $1\frac{1}{4}$ bags of balloons to decorate the room. How many balloons did she use?

4. For the party, Jeff's mother bought sandwich trays from the Servin' Sandwiches Shop. Each tray contained 9 sandwiches. The party guests left $\frac{2}{3}$ of a tray of sandwiches. How many sandwiches did they leave?

5. To make a pitcher of lemonade, Jeff needed 8 cups of water. He could only find a $\frac{1}{3}$-cup measuring cup. How many times did Jeff fill the $\frac{1}{3}$-cup when he made the lemonade?

6. One-half of Jeff's guests were relatives. Three-fifths of the relatives were cousins.
   A. What fraction of his guests were cousins?
   B. Jeff had 20 guests at his party. How many of the guests were cousins?

Student Guide - page 392 (Answers on p. 85)

7. Jeff's family spent $77.50 on the party. If there were 20 guests at the party, about how much money did they spend on each guest?

8. It was very cold when the guests arrived at the party. The temperature was -5°F. When the guests left, the temperature was -17°F. What was the difference between the two temperatures?

9. Jeff had a total of 43 favors to give to his guests. If each guest got the same number of favors, how many favors did each guest take home? How many favors were left over?

10. Jeff's mother created a riddle for the guests to solve:

    Today is also Jeff's uncle's birthday. His age has 2 and 5 as some of its factors; 3 is not a factor. His age is more than the square of 7 but less than the square of 8.
    A. Is Jeff's uncle's age prime or composite?
    B. What is the square of 7? of 8?
    C. What is Jeff's uncle's age?

Student Guide - page 393 (Answers on p. 85)

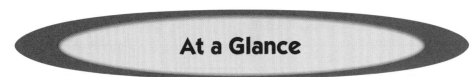

At a Glance

Teaching the Activity

Students complete *Questions 1–10* on the *Party Problems* Activity Pages in the *Student Guide.*

Homework

Assign some or all of the problems for homework.

Answer Key is on page 85.

Notes:

Student Guide (pp. 392–393)

Party Problems

Solution strategies will vary for *Questions 1–10.*

1. $\frac{3}{5}$

2. 15 cups. There are $18 \times \frac{1}{6} = 3$ cups left. Therefore, the guests drank $18 - 3 = 15$ cups of lemonade.

3. 10 balloons; 1 bag has 8 balloons; $\frac{1}{4}$ bag has $\frac{1}{4} \times 8 = 2$ balloons. So, $1\frac{1}{4}$ bags have $8 + 2 = 10$ balloons.

4. 6 sandwiches; $9 \times \frac{2}{3} = 6$

5. 24 times

6. **A.** $\frac{3}{10}$ cousins; $\frac{3}{5} \times \frac{1}{2} = \frac{3}{10}$
   B. 6; $\frac{3}{10} \times 20 = 6$

7. Estimates will vary. One possible solution is $\$80 \div 20 = \$4$.

8. 12°F

9. Each guest got 2 favors with 3 favors left over; $43 \div 20 = 2$ R3.

10. **A.** Composite, since it has 2 and 5 as some of its factors.
    B. $7^2 = 49$ and $8^2 = 64$
    C. 50 years old. If a number has both 2 and 5 as factors, 10 is also a factor. The multiples of 10 between 49 and 64 are 50 and 60. Jeff's uncle's age is 50 since 3 is a factor of 60, but not of 50.

Party Problems

Solve the following problems. Show how you solved each problem.

HAPPY BIRTHDAY

1. Jeff's sister made a HAPPY BIRTHDAY sign for Jeff. Since Jeff is 10 years old, his sister drew 10 flowers. She colored $\frac{2}{5}$ of the flowers yellow and the rest she colored red. What fraction of the flowers are red?

2. At the beginning of the party, Jeff set 18 cups of lemonade on the table. After the party was over, $\frac{1}{6}$ of the cups of lemonade were left. How many cups of lemonade did Jeff's guests drink?

3. Jeff's mother bought 2 bags of balloons. Each bag contained 8 balloons. She used $1\frac{1}{4}$ bags of balloons to decorate the room. How many balloons did she use?

4. For the party, Jeff's mother bought sandwich trays from the Servin' Sandwiches Shop. Each tray contained 9 sandwiches. The party guests left $\frac{2}{3}$ of a tray of sandwiches. How many sandwiches did they leave?

5. To make a pitcher of lemonade, Jeff needed 8 cups of water. He could only find a $\frac{1}{3}$-cup measuring cup. How many times did Jeff fill the $\frac{1}{3}$-cup when he made the lemonade?

6. One-half of Jeff's guests were relatives. Three-fifths of the relatives were cousins.
   A. What fraction of his guests were cousins?
   B. Jeff had 20 guests at his party. How many of the guests were cousins?

392   SG • Grade 5 • Unit 12 • Lesson 7   Party Problems

Student Guide - page 392

7. Jeff's family spent $77.50 on the party. If there were 20 guests at the party, about how much money did they spend on each guest?

8. It was very cold when the guests arrived at the party. The temperature was -5°F. When the guests left, the temperature was -17°F. What was the difference between the two temperatures?

9. Jeff had a total of 43 favors to give to his guests. If each guest got the same number of favors, how many favors did each guest take home? How many favors were left over?

10. Jeff's mother created a riddle for the guests to solve:

    Today is also Jeff's uncle's birthday. His age has 2 and 5 as some of its factors; 3 is not a factor. His age is more than the square of 7 but less than the square of 8.
    A. Is Jeff's uncle's age prime or composite?
    B. What is the square of 7? of 8?
    C. What is Jeff's uncle's age?

Party Problems   SG • Grade 5 • Unit 12 • Lesson 7   393

Student Guide - page 393

Lesson 8

Midterm Test

Estimated Class Sessions

1

Lesson Overview

Students take a paper-and-pencil test consisting of 14 items. These items test skills and concepts studied in Units 9 through 12.

Key Content

- Assessing concepts and skills developed in Units 9 through 12.

Math Facts

DPP Bit M reviews the last six facts.

Homework

1. Assign DPP Task N for homework.
2. Assign Part 7 of the Home Practice.

Assessment

Add this test to students' portfolios to compare to similar assessments.

Materials List

Supplies and Copies

Student	Teacher
Supplies for Each Student • pattern blocks • ruler • calculator	**Supplies**
Copies • 1 copy of *Midterm Test* per student (*Unit Resource Guide* Pages 91–96)	**Copies/Transparencies**

All blackline masters including assessment, transparency, and DPP masters are also on the Teacher Resource CD.

Daily Practice and Problems and Home Practice

DPP items M–N (*Unit Resource Guide* Page 19)
Home Practice Part 7 (*Discovery Assignment Book* Page 192)

Note: Classrooms whose pacing differs significantly from the suggested pacing of the units should use the Math Facts Calendar in Section 4 of the *Facts Resource Guide* to ensure students receive the complete math facts program.

Daily Practice and Problems

Suggestions for using the DPPs are on page 89.

M. Bit: Fact Practice (URG p. 19)

A. $60 \times 80 =$

B. $420 \div 70 =$

C. $32,000 \div 400 =$

D. $70 \times 8 =$

E. $2400 \div 6 =$

F. $7000 \times 40 =$

N. Task: Inheriting Money
(URG p. 19)

Krista's uncle died and left her his money. To claim her fortune, she has to solve this riddle that tells the amount she inherited.

Take your time to find a prime.

But, beware, it's one more than a square.

It's under one hundred and ends in seven.

Now, add six zeros and you'll be in heaven.

Problems, you say, there's more than
    one solution?

Then, add them, my dear, and enjoy
    your fortune.

How much money did Krista inherit?

Teaching the Activity

Students take the test individually. Although the test is designed for students to complete in one class session, you may wish to give them more time. Part 1 of the test consists of 2 division problems. These are included to assess students' fluency with paper-and-pencil methods for division. Students should complete these items without using a calculator. Once students complete these items, they should have calculators, rulers, and pattern blocks readily available for the remaining problems in Part 2.

Ask students to follow the directions for each item. Some items ask students to tell how they solved the problem. Encourage them to give full explanations of the solving process used.

Math Facts

DPP Bit M reviews the last six facts with multiples of ten.

Homework and Practice

- Assign DPP Task N that involves solving a riddle.
- Assign Home Practice Part 7.

Answers for Part 7 of the Home Practice are in the Answer Key at the end of this lesson and at the end of this unit.

Assessment

Add this test to students' portfolios so you can compare students' performance on this test to their performance on similar activities throughout the year.

Name _____   Date _____

PART 7 Food for Thought

Solve the following problems. You may use any of the tools you have used in class such as calculators, drawings, or pattern blocks. Show your solutions.

1. A. If three friends split $1\frac{1}{2}$ pizzas evenly, how much of a whole pizza will each person eat?

   B. If six friends split $1\frac{1}{2}$ pizzas, how much of a whole pizza will each person eat?

2. Michael's father made a pumpkin pie. Michael and his brother couldn't wait until after dinner to eat the pie. Michael ate $\frac{1}{8}$ of the pie. His brother ate $\frac{1}{4}$ of the pie. What fraction of the whole pie was left for dessert after dinner?

3. Ana is making nut bread for a bake sale. The recipe for one loaf of bread calls for $\frac{3}{4}$ cup of nuts. If she wants to make 5 loaves of bread, how many cups of nuts does she need?

4. David is making orange punch. He combines $5\frac{1}{4}$ cups of orange juice with $2\frac{2}{3}$ cups of sparkling water. Can he pour all the punch into a 2-quart pitcher? Why or why not? (1 quart = 4 cups)

5. A muffin recipe calls for $\frac{1}{3}$ cup of blueberries for each pan of muffins. If Blanca picked 3 cups of berries, how many pans of muffins can Blanca make?

192 DAB • Grade 5 • Unit 12   USING FRACTIONS

Discovery Assignment Book **- page 192** *(Answers on p. 97)*

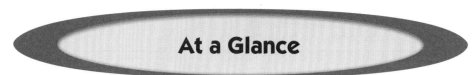

At a Glance

Math Facts and Daily Practice and Problems

DPP Bit M reviews the last six facts. Task N involves problem solving.

Teaching the Activity

1. Students complete Part 1 of the *Midterm Test* without a calculator.
2. Students complete Part 2 of the test. Make available calculators, rulers, and pattern blocks.

Homework

1. Assign DPP Task N for homework.
2. Assign Part 7 of the Home Practice.

Assessment

Add this test to students' portfolios to compare to similar assessments.

Answer Key is on pages 97–100.

Notes:

Midterm Test

Part 1

Solve Questions 1 and 2 using a paper-and-pencil method to divide. Write any remainders as whole numbers. Check your work using multiplication.

1. 17) 982

2. 24) 2694

Name _____ Date _____

Part 2

As you answer questions on this part of the test, you may use any tools you used in class. For example, you may use a calculator, a ruler, and pattern blocks.

3. Mr. Moreno traveled 455 miles in a two-week period. What is the average number of miles he traveled each day?

4. **A.** Mr. Moreno bought and used 42 gallons of fuel for $58.38 during the two-week period. If Mr. Moreno traveled about the same number of miles each day, <u>estimate</u> the average cost of fuel each day.

   B. About how many miles can Mr. Moreno travel on one gallon of fuel?

5. Mr. Moreno and his wife went on a road trip. They decided to switch drivers every 75 miles. If the road trip lasted 889 miles, how many times did they switch drivers?

6. Use exponents to rename each number below as a product of its prime factors. Organize your work in a factor tree.

A. 315

B. 440

7. Reduce each fraction to lowest terms.

A. $\frac{12}{18} =$ _____

B. $\frac{8}{32} =$ _____

C. $\frac{9}{24} =$ _____

8. Rename each decimal as a fraction. Reduce the fraction to lowest terms.

A. $0.8 =$ _____

B. $0.75 =$ _____

C. Write this fraction as a decimal: $\frac{15}{24} =$ _____

9. A. Using the coordinates given, plot the shape below.

  B. Write the ordered pairs in the table.

Ordered Pair	*x*-coordinate	*y*-coordinate
	-1	1
	1	1
	3	3
	1	3

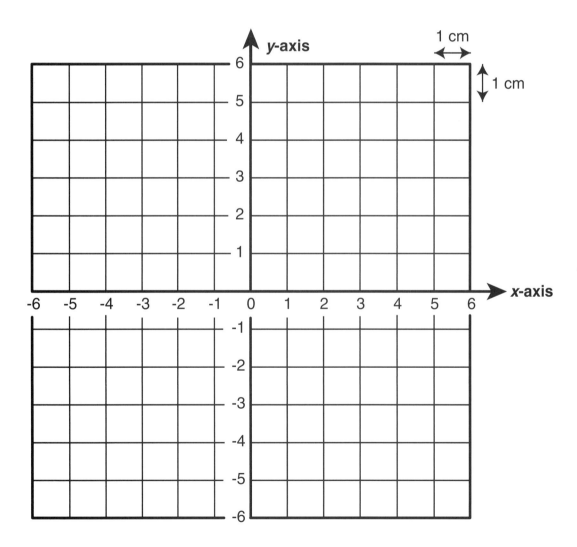

10. Garbage collectors drop off waste at two sites each day. One site collects nonrecyclable waste while the other site collects recyclable waste. The map below shows the two sites.

　　A. Write the coordinates for each site on the map.

　　B. Use the map to find the actual distance between the sites.

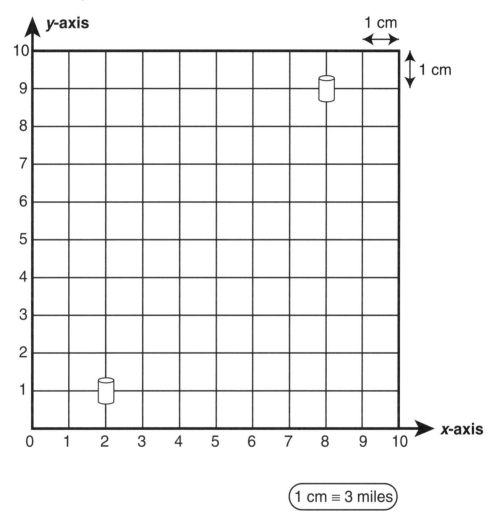

1 cm ≡ 3 miles

11. The Johnny Appleseed Company has decided to sell a special gift box of apples with 18 apples. If $\frac{2}{3}$ of the apples are red, how many of the apples are red? Show how you solved the problem.

12. Solve $\frac{1}{4} \times \frac{2}{3}$ following these steps:

- Solve the problem and write a number sentence. Be sure your answer is in lowest terms.

- Record your work on the diagram below.

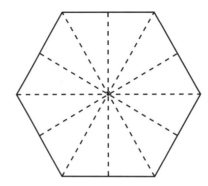

13. To make cookies, David mixed $3\frac{3}{4}$ cups of flour with $1\frac{2}{3}$ cups of sugar in a bowl. How many cups of flour and sugar did David have in the bowl? Show how you solved the problem.

14. Complete the following problems. Give your answer in lowest terms.

A. $\frac{1}{6} + \frac{2}{9} =$

B. $\frac{5}{8} - \frac{3}{8} =$

C. $\frac{1}{15} + \frac{3}{5} =$

Discovery Assignment Book (p. 192)

Home Practice*

Part 7. Food for Thought

1. **A.** $\frac{1}{2}$ pizza

   B. $\frac{1}{4}$ pizza

2. $\frac{5}{8}$ of the pie

3. $3\frac{3}{4}$ cups

4. Yes; the punch is $5\frac{1}{4} + 2\frac{2}{3} = 7\frac{11}{12}$ cups. Since 2 quarts is 8 cups and the punch is only $7\frac{11}{12}$ cups, David can pour all the punch into a 2-quart pitcher.

5. 9 pans of muffins

Name _____ Date _____

PART 7 Food for Thought

Solve the following problems. You may use any of the tools you have used in class such as calculators, drawings, or pattern blocks. Show your solutions.

1. **A.** If three friends split $1\frac{1}{2}$ pizzas evenly, how much of a whole pizza will each person eat?

   B. If six friends split $1\frac{1}{2}$ pizzas, how much of a whole pizza will each person eat?

2. Michael's father made a pumpkin pie. Michael and his brother couldn't wait until after dinner to eat the pie. Michael ate $\frac{1}{8}$ of the pie. His brother ate $\frac{1}{4}$ of the pie. What fraction of the whole pie was left for dessert after dinner?

3. Ana is making nut bread for a bake sale. The recipe for one loaf of bread calls for $\frac{3}{4}$ cup of nuts. If she wants to make 5 loaves of bread, how many cups of nuts does she need?

4. David is making orange punch. He combines $5\frac{1}{4}$ cups of orange juice with $2\frac{2}{3}$ cups of sparkling water. Can he pour all the punch into a 2-quart pitcher? Why or why not? (1 quart = 4 cups)

5. A muffin recipe calls for $\frac{1}{3}$ cup of blueberries for each pan of muffins. If Blanca picked 3 cups of berries, how many pans of muffins can Blanca make?

192 DAB • Grade 5 • Unit 12   USING FRACTIONS

Discovery Assignment Book **- page 192**

Unit Resource Guide (p. 91)

Midterm Test

1. 57 R13

2. 112 R6

Name _____ Date _____

Midterm Test

Part 1

Solve Questions 1 and 2 using a paper-and-pencil method to divide. Write any remainders as whole numbers. Check your work using multiplication.

1. $17\overline{\smash{)}982}$

2. $24\overline{\smash{)}2694}$

Assessment Blackline Master   URG • Grade 5 • Unit 12 • Lesson 8   **91**

Unit Resource Guide **- page 91**

*Answers for all the Home Practice in the *Discovery Assignment Book* are at the end of the unit.

Name _____ Date _____

Part 2

As you answer questions on this part of the test, you may use any tools you used in class. For example, you may use a calculator, a ruler, and pattern blocks.

3. Mr. Moreno traveled 455 miles in a two-week period. What is the average number of miles he traveled each day?

4. **A.** Mr. Moreno bought and used 42 gallons of fuel for $58.38 during the two-week period. If Mr. Moreno traveled about the same number of miles each day, <u>estimate</u> the average cost of fuel each day.

   B. About how many miles can Mr. Moreno travel on one gallon of fuel?

5. Mr. Moreno and his wife went on a road trip. They decided to switch drivers every 75 miles. If the road trip lasted 889 miles, how many times did they switch drivers?

Copyright © Kendall/Hunt Publishing Company

92   URG • Grade 5 • Unit 12 • Lesson 8   Assessment Blackline Master

Unit Resource Guide - page 92

Name _____ Date _____

6. Use exponents to rename each number below as a product of its prime factors. Organize your work in a factor tree.

   A. 315   **B.** 440

7. Reduce each fraction to lowest terms.

   A. $\frac{12}{18}$ = _____

   B. $\frac{8}{32}$ = _____

   C. $\frac{9}{24}$ = _____

8. Rename each decimal as a fraction. Reduce the fraction to lowest terms.

   A. 0.8 = _____

   B. 0.75 = _____

   C. Write this fraction as a decimal: $\frac{15}{24}$ = _____

Copyright © Kendall/Hunt Publishing Company

Assessment Blackline Master   URG • Grade 5 • Unit 12 • Lesson 8   93

Unit Resource Guide - page 93

Unit Resource Guide (pp. 92–93)

3. $32\frac{1}{2}$ miles or 32.5 miles

4. **A.** About $4

   B. About 10 or 11 miles

5. 11 times

6. **A.** $315 = 3^2 \times 5 \times 7$. Factor trees will vary. One possible solution is shown.

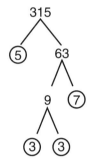

   B. $440 = 2^3 \times 5 \times 11$. Factor trees will vary. One possible solution is shown.

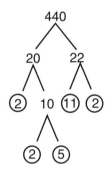

7. **A.** $\frac{2}{3}$ **B.** $\frac{1}{4}$ **C.** $\frac{3}{8}$

8. **A.** $\frac{8}{10} = \frac{4}{5}$ **B.** $\frac{75}{100} = \frac{3}{4}$ **C.** 0.625

Unit Resource Guide (pp. 94–95)

9. A.

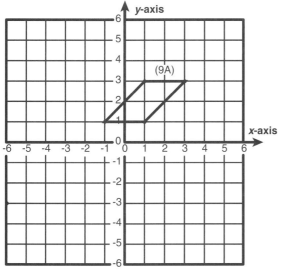

B.

Ordered Pair	*x*-coordinate	*y*-coordinate
(-1, 1)	-1	1
(1, 1)	1	1
(3, 3)	3	3
(1, 3)	1	3

10. (2, 1), (8, 9). The sites are 10 cm apart. Using the scale, this is 30 miles.

11. 12. Solution strategies will vary.

$\frac{2}{3} \times 18 = 12$ apples

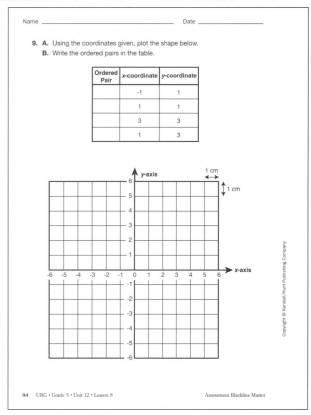

Unit Resource Guide - page 94

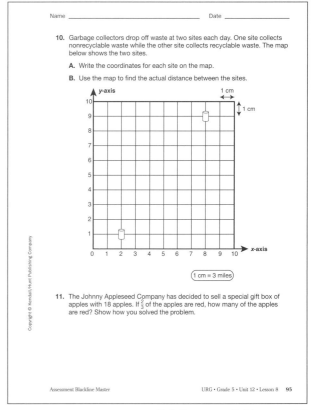

Unit Resource Guide - page 95

Name _____ Date _____

12. Solve $\frac{1}{4} \times \frac{2}{3}$ following these steps:

• Solve the problem and write a number sentence. Be sure your answer is in lowest terms.

• Record your work on the diagram below.

13. To make cookies, David mixed $3\frac{3}{4}$ cups of flour with $1\frac{2}{3}$ cups of sugar in a bowl. How many cups of flour and sugar did David have in the bowl? Show how you solved the problem.

14. Complete the following problems. Give your answer in lowest terms.

A. $\frac{1}{6} + \frac{2}{9} =$

B. $\frac{5}{8} - \frac{3}{8} =$

C. $\frac{1}{15} + \frac{3}{5} =$

Copyright © Kendall/Hunt Publishing Company

Assessment Blackline Master

Unit Resource Guide **- page 96**

Unit Resource Guide (p. 96)

12.

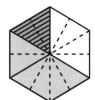

$$\frac{1}{4} \times \frac{2}{3} = \frac{1 \times 2}{4 \times 3} = \frac{2}{12} = \frac{1}{6}$$

13. $5\frac{5}{12}$

14. A. $\frac{7}{18}$ **B.** $\frac{1}{4}$ **C.** $\frac{2}{3}$

Discovery Assignment Book (p. 189)

Part 1. Multiplication and Division Practice

I. A. $1494\frac{1}{2}$ B. $117\frac{1}{2}$

C. 2214 D. 80

E. 420

2. Answers will vary: Possible response for 1E: $105 \times 4 = 100 \times 4 + 5 \times 4 = 400 + 20 = 420$

Part 2. Division Practice

I. A. $8\frac{1}{4}$ B. $8\frac{4}{9}$

C. $8\frac{1}{2}$ D. $10\frac{8}{10} = 10\frac{4}{5}$

E. $7\frac{5}{7}$ F. $6\frac{5}{6}$

G. $5\frac{2}{8} = 5\frac{1}{4}$ H. $3\frac{5}{6}$

I. $8\frac{3}{8}$

2. A. $86\frac{12}{16} = 86\frac{3}{4}$

B. $769\frac{22}{24} = 769\frac{11}{12}$

C. $1373\frac{20}{32} = 1373\frac{5}{8}$

Discovery Assignment Book - page 189

Discovery Assignment Book (p. 190)

Part 3. Fractions

I. A. 5 B. 3

C. $\frac{1}{9}$ D. $\frac{1}{6}$

E. $\frac{1}{30}$ F. 6

G. $50¢$ H. $\$20$

I. $\$18$

2. Two possible strategies: $\frac{1}{5} \times \frac{5}{6} = \frac{5}{30} = \frac{1}{6}$; $\frac{1}{5}$ of 5 is 1, so $\frac{1}{5}$ of $\frac{5}{6}$ is $\frac{1}{6}$.

Part 4. Analyze the Class

I. 6 2. 8

3. $\frac{3}{4}$ 4. 75%

5. $\frac{1}{2}$

Discovery Assignment Book - page 190

Name _____ Date _____

PART 5 Let's Practice

Use paper and pencil to solve the following. Use a separate sheet of paper to show your work.

A. $3\frac{4}{5} + 7\frac{1}{4} =$ B. $862 \times 9 =$ C. $94 \times 34 =$

D. $53.68 + 0.432 =$ E. $7341 \div 9 =$ F. $82 - 14.65 =$

PART 6 Working with Coordinates

I. A. Plot the coordinates in the table. Record the ordered pairs. Label the points with a letter on the graph.

Point	x-coordinate	y-coordinate	Ordered Pairs
A	-2	-1	
B	-3	-3	
C	-1	-3	
D	1	3	

B. You will need a ruler for this problem.
If 1 cm = 200 cm on the graph, what is the distance between A and D?

Discovery Assignment Book - page 191

Name _____ Date _____

PART 7 Food for Thought

Solve the following problems. You may use any of the tools you have used in class such as calculators, drawings, or pattern blocks. Show your solutions.

I. A. If three friends split $1\frac{1}{2}$ pizzas evenly, how much of a whole pizza will each person eat?

B. If six friends split $1\frac{1}{2}$ pizzas, how much of a whole pizza will each person eat?

2. Michael's father made a pumpkin pie. Michael and his brother couldn't wait until after dinner to eat the pie. Michael ate $\frac{1}{8}$ of the pie. His brother ate $\frac{1}{4}$ of the pie. What fraction of the whole pie was left for dessert after dinner?

3. Ana is making nut bread for a bake sale. The recipe for one loaf of bread calls for $\frac{3}{4}$ cup of nuts. If she wants to make 5 loaves of bread, how many cups of nuts does she need?

4. David is making orange punch. He combines $5\frac{1}{4}$ cups of orange juice with $2\frac{2}{3}$ cups of sparkling water. Can he pour all the punch into a 2-quart pitcher? Why or why not? (1 quart = 4 cups)

5. A muffin recipe calls for $\frac{1}{3}$ cup of blueberries for each pan of muffins. If Blanca picked 3 cups of berries, how many pans of muffins can Blanca make?

Discovery Assignment Book - page 192

Discovery Assignment Book (pp. 191–192)

Part 5. Let's Practice

A. $11\frac{1}{20}$ B. 7758

C. 3196   D. 54.112

E. 815 R6 or $815\frac{2}{3}$ F. 67.35

Part 6. Working with Coordinates

I. A.

Point	x-coordinate	y-coordinate	Ordered Pair
A	-2	-1	(-2, -1)
B	-3	-3	(-3, -3)
C	-1	-3	(-1, -3)
D	1	3	(1, 3)

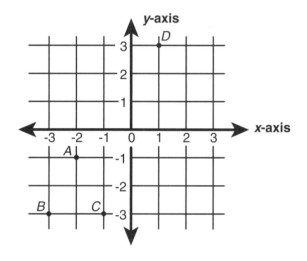

B. 1000 cm

Part 7. Food for Thought

I. A. $\frac{1}{2}$ pizza

B. $\frac{1}{4}$ pizza

2. $\frac{5}{8}$ of the pie

3. $3\frac{3}{4}$ cups

4. Yes; the punch is $5\frac{1}{4} + 2\frac{2}{3} = 7\frac{11}{12}$ cups. Since 2 quarts is 8 cups and the punch is only $7\frac{11}{12}$ cups, David can pour all the punch into a 2-quart pitcher.

5. 9 pans of muffins

Glossary

This glossary provides definitions of key vocabulary terms in the Grade 5 lessons. Locations of key vocabulary terms in the curriculum are included with each definition. Components Key: URG = *Unit Resource Guide* and SG = *Student Guide*.

A

Acute Angle (URG Unit 6; SG Unit 6)
An angle that measures less than 90°.

Acute Triangle (URG Unit 6 & Unit 15; SG Unit 6 & Unit 15)
A triangle that has only acute angles.

All-Partials Multiplication Method (URG Unit 2)
A paper-and-pencil method for solving multiplication problems. Each partial product is recorded on a separate line. (*See also* partial product.)

$$\begin{array}{r} 186 \\ \times\ 3 \\ \hline 18 \\ 240 \\ 300 \\ \hline 558 \end{array}$$

Altitude of a Triangle (URG Unit 15; SG Unit 15)
A line segment from a vertex of a triangle perpendicular to the opposite side or to the line extending the opposite side; also, the length of this line. The altitude is also called the height of the triangle.

Angle (URG Unit 6; SG Unit 6)
The amount of turning or the amount of opening between two rays that have the same endpoint.

Arc (URG Unit 14; SG Unit 14)
Part of a circle between two points. (*See also* circle.)

Area (URG Unit 4 & Unit 15; SG Unit 4 & Unit 15)
A measurement of size. The area of a shape is the amount of space it covers, measured in square units.

Average (URG Unit 1 & Unit 4; SG Unit 1 & Unit 4)
A number that can be used to represent a typical value in a set of data. (*See also* mean, median, and mode.)

Axes (URG Unit 10; SG Unit 10)
Reference lines on a graph. In the Cartesian coordinate system, the axes are two perpendicular lines that meet at the origin. The singular of axes is axis.

B

Base of a Triangle (URG Unit 15; SG Unit 15)
One of the sides of a triangle; also, the length of the side. A perpendicular line drawn from the vertex opposite the base is called the height or altitude of the triangle.

Base of an Exponent (URG Unit 2; SG Unit 2)
When exponents are used, the number being multiplied. In $3^4 = 3 \times 3 \times 3 \times 3 = 81$, the 3 is the base and the 4 is the exponent. The 3 is multiplied by itself 4 times.

Base-Ten Pieces (URG Unit 2; SG Unit 2)
A set of manipulatives used to model our number system as shown in the figure below. Note that a skinny is made of 10 bits, a flat is made of 100 bits, and a pack is made of 1000 bits.

Base-Ten Shorthand (URG Unit 2)
A graphical representation of the base-ten pieces as shown below.

Nickname	Picture	Shorthand
bit	⬚	•
skinny	▭▭▭▭▭	/
flat	▱	▱
pack	▦	▱

Benchmarks (SG Unit 7)
Numbers convenient for comparing and ordering numbers, e.g., $0, \frac{1}{2}, 1$ are convenient benchmarks for comparing and ordering fractions.

Best-Fit Line (URG Unit 3; SG Unit 3)
The line that comes closest to the points on a point graph.

Binning Data (URG Unit 8; SG Unit 8)
Placing data from a data set with a large number of values or large range into intervals in order to more easily see patterns in the data.

Bit (URG Unit 2; SG Unit 2)
A cube that measures 1 cm on each edge.
It is the smallest of the base-ten pieces and is often used to represent 1. (*See also* base-ten pieces.)

C

Cartesian Coordinate System (URG Unit 10; SG Unit 10)
A method of locating points on a flat surface by means of an ordered pair of numbers. This method is named after its originator, René Descartes. (*See also* coordinates.)

Categorical Variable (URG Unit 1; SG Unit 1)
Variables with values that are not numbers. (*See also* variable and value.)

Center of a Circle (URG Unit 14; SG Unit 14)
The point such that every point on a circle is the same distance from it. (*See also* circle.)

Centiwheel (URG Unit 7; SG Unit 7)
A circle divided into 100 equal sections used in exploring fractions, decimals, and percents.

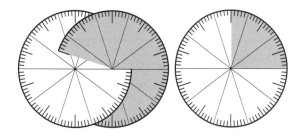

Central Angle (URG Unit 14; SG Unit 14)
An angle whose vertex is at the center of a circle.

Certain Event (URG Unit 7; SG Unit 7)
An event that has a probability of 1 (100%).

Chord (URG Unit 14; SG Unit 14)
A line segment that connects two points on a circle. (*See also* circle.)

Circle (URG Unit 14; SG Unit 14)
A curve that is made up of all the points that are the same distance from one point, the center.

Circumference (URG Unit 14; SG Unit 14)
The distance around a circle.

Common Denominator (URG Unit 5 & Unit 11; SG Unit 5 & Unit 11)
A denominator that is shared by two or more fractions. A common denominator is a common multiple of the denominators of the fractions. 15 is a common denominator of $\frac{2}{3} (= \frac{10}{15})$ and $\frac{4}{5} (= \frac{12}{15})$ since 15 is divisible by both 3 and 5.

Common Fraction (URG Unit 7; SG Unit 7)
Any fraction that is written with a numerator and denominator that are whole numbers. For example, $\frac{3}{4}$ and $\frac{9}{4}$ are both common fractions. (*See also* decimal fraction.)

Commutative Property of Addition (URG Unit 2)
The order of the addends in an addition problem does not matter, e.g., $7 + 3 = 3 + 7$.

Commutative Property of Multiplication (URG Unit 2)
The order of the factors in a multiplication problem does not matter, e.g., $7 \times 3 = 3 \times 7$. (*See also* turn-around facts.)

Compact Method (URG Unit 2)
Another name for what is considered the traditional multiplication algorithm.
$$\begin{array}{r} {\scriptstyle 2\,1} \\ 186 \\ \times\ 3 \\ \hline 558 \end{array}$$

Composite Number (URG Unit 11; SG Unit 11)
A number that has more than two distinct factors. For example, 9 has three factors (1, 3, 9) so it is a composite number.

Concentric Circles (URG Unit 14; SG Unit 14)
Circles that have the same center.

Congruent (URG Unit 6 & Unit 10; SG Unit 6)
Figures that are the same shape and size. Polygons are congruent when corresponding sides have the same length and corresponding angles have the same measure.

Conjecture (URG Unit 11; SG Unit 11)
A statement that has not been proved to be true, nor shown to be false.

Convenient Number (URG Unit 2; SG Unit 2)
A number used in computation that is close enough to give a good estimate, but is also easy to compute with mentally, e.g., 25 and 30 are convenient numbers for 27.

Convex (URG Unit 6)
A shape is convex if for any two points in the shape, the line segment between the points is also inside the shape.

Coordinates (URG Unit 10; SG Unit 10)
An ordered pair of numbers that locates points on a flat surface relative to a pair of coordinate axes. For example, in the ordered pair (4, 5), the first number (coordinate) is the distance from the point to the vertical axis and the second coordinate is the distance from the point to the horizontal axis. (*See also* axes.)

Corresponding Parts (URG Unit 10; SG Unit 10)
Matching parts in two or more figures. In the figure below, Sides AB and A′B′ are corresponding parts.

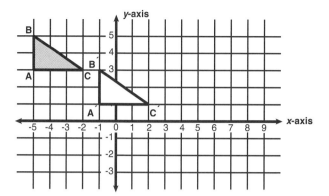

Cryptography (SG Unit 11) The study of secret codes.

Cubic Centimeter (URG Unit 13)
The volume of a cube that is one centimeter long on each edge.

D

Data (SG Unit 1)
Information collected in an experiment or survey.

Decagon (URG Unit 6; SG Unit 6)
A ten-sided, ten-angled polygon.

Decimal (URG Unit 7; SG Unit 7)
1. A number written using the base ten place value system.
2. A number containing a decimal point.

Decimal Fraction (URG Unit 7; SG Unit 7)
A fraction written as a decimal. For example, 0.75 and 0.4 are decimal fractions and $\frac{75}{100}$ and $\frac{4}{10}$ are the equivalent common fractions.

Degree (URG Unit 6; SG Unit 6)
A degree (°) is a unit of measure for angles. There are 360 degrees in a circle.

Denominator (URG Unit 3; SG Unit 3)
The number below the line in a fraction. The denominator indicates the number of equal parts in which the unit whole is divided. For example, the 5 is the denominator in the fraction $\frac{2}{5}$. In this case the unit whole is divided into five equal parts. (*See also* numerator.)

Density (URG Unit 13; SG Unit 13)
The ratio of an object's mass to its volume.

Diagonal (URG Unit 6)
A line segment that connects nonadjacent corners of a polygon.

Diameter (URG Unit 14; SG Unit 14)
1. A line segment that connects two points on a circle and passes through the center.
2. The length of this line segment.

Digit (SG Unit 2)
Any one of the ten symbols 0, 1, 2, 3, 4, 5, 6, 7, 8, 9. The number 37 is made up of the digits 3 and 7.

Dividend (URG Unit 4 & Unit 9; SG Unit 4 & Unit 9)
The number that is divided in a division problem, e.g., 12 is the dividend in 12 ÷ 3 = 4.

Divisor (URG Unit 2, Unit 4, & Unit 9; SG Unit 2, Unit 4, & Unit 9)
In a division problem, the number by which another number is divided. In the problem 12 ÷ 4 = 3, the 4 is the divisor, the 12 is the dividend, and the 3 is the quotient.

Dodecagon (URG Unit 6; SG Unit 6)
A twelve-sided, twelve-angled polygon.

E

Endpoint (URG Unit 6; SG Unit 6)
The point at either end of a line segment or the point at the end of a ray.

Equally Likely (URG Unit 7; SG Unit 7)
When events have the same probability, they are called equally likely.

Equidistant (URG Unit 14)
At the same distance.

Equilateral Triangle (URG Unit 6, Unit 14, & Unit 15)
A triangle that has all three sides equal in length. An equilateral triangle also has three equal angles.

Equivalent Fractions (URG Unit 3; SG Unit 3)
Fractions that have the same value, e.g., $\frac{2}{4} = \frac{1}{2}$.

Estimate (URG Unit 2; SG Unit 2)
1. To find *about* how many (as a verb).
2. A number that is *close to* the desired number (as a noun).

Expanded Form (SG Unit 2)
A way to write numbers that shows the place value of each digit, e.g., 4357 = 4000 + 300 + 50 + 7.

Exponent (URG Unit 2 & Unit 11; SG Unit 2 & Unit 11)
The number of times the base is multiplied by itself. In $3^4 = 3 \times 3 \times 3 \times 3 = 81$, the 3 is the base and the 4 is the exponent. The 3 is multiplied by itself 4 times.

Extrapolation (URG Unit 13; SG Unit 13)
Using patterns in data to make predictions or to estimate values that lie beyond the range of values in the set of data.

F

Fact Families (URG Unit 2; SG Unit 2)
Related math facts, e.g., 3 × 4 = 12, 4 × 3 = 12, 12 ÷ 3 = 4, 12 ÷ 4 = 3.

Factor Tree (URG Unit 11; SG Unit 11)
A diagram that shows the prime factorization of a number.

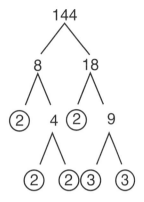

Factors (URG Unit 2 & Unit 11; SG Unit 2 & Unit 11)
1. In a multiplication problem, the numbers that are multiplied together. In the problem $3 \times 4 = 12$, 3 and 4 are the factors.
2. Numbers that divide a number evenly, e.g., 1, 2, 3, 4, 6, and 12 are all the factors of 12.

Fair Game (URG Unit 7; SG Unit 7)
A game in which it is equally likely that any player will win.

Fewest Pieces Rule (URG Unit 2)
Using the least number of base-ten pieces to represent a number. (*See also* base-ten pieces.)

Fixed Variables (URG Unit 4; SG Unit 3 & Unit 4)
Variables in an experiment that are held constant or not changed, in order to find the relationship between the manipulated and responding variables. These variables are often called controlled variables. (*See also* manipulated variable and responding variable.)

Flat (URG Unit 2; SG Unit 2)
A block that measures 1 cm $\times$ 10 cm $\times$ 10 cm. It is one of the base-ten pieces and is often used to represent 100. (*See also* base-ten pieces.)

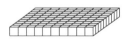

Flip (URG Unit 10; SG Unit 10)
A motion of the plane in which the plane is reflected over a line so that any point and its image are the same distance from the line.

Forgiving Division Method
(URG Unit 4; SG Unit 4)
A paper-and-pencil method for division in which successive partial quotients are chosen and subtracted from the dividend, until the remainder is less than the divisor. The sum of the partial quotients is the quotient. For example, $644 \div 7$ can be solved as shown at the right.

```
        92
   7 ⟌ 644
      140  20
      ———
      504
      350  50
      ———
      154
      140  20
      ———
       14
       14   2
      ———
        0  92
```

Formula (SG Unit 11 & Unit 14)
A number sentence that gives a general rule. A formula for finding the area of a rectangle is Area = length $\times$ width, or $A = l \times w$.

Fraction (URG Unit 7; SG Unit 7)
A number that can be written as a/b where a and b are whole numbers and b is not zero.

G

Googol (URG Unit 2)
A number that is written as a 1 with 100 zeroes after it (10^{100}).

Googolplex (URG Unit 2)
A number that is written as a 1 with a googol of zeroes after it.

H

Height of a Triangle (URG Unit 15; SG Unit 15)
A line segment from a vertex of a triangle perpendicular to the opposite side or to the line extending the opposite side; also, the length of this line. The height is also called the altitude.

Hexagon (URG Unit 6; SG Unit 6)
A six-sided polygon.

Hypotenuse (URG Unit 15; SG Unit 15)
The longest side of a right triangle.

I

Image (URG Unit 10; SG Unit 10)
The result of a transformation, in particular a slide (translation) or a flip (reflection), in a coordinate plane. The new figure after the slide or flip is the image of the old figure.

Impossible Event (URG Unit 7; SG Unit 7)
An event that has a probability of 0 or 0%.

Improper Fraction (URG Unit 3; SG Unit 3)
A fraction in which the numerator is greater than or equal to the denominator. An improper fraction is greater than or equal to one.

Infinite (URG Unit 2)
Never ending, immeasurably great, unlimited.

Interpolation (URG Unit 13; SG Unit 13)
Making predictions or estimating values that lie between data points in a set of data.

Intersect (URG Unit 14)
To meet or cross.

Isosceles Triangle (URG Unit 6 & Unit 15)
A triangle that has at least two sides of equal length.

J

K

L

Lattice Multiplication
(URG Unit 9; SG Unit 9)
A method for multiplying that
uses a lattice to arrange the
partial products so the digits are
correctly placed in the correct
place value columns. A lattice
for 43 × 96 = 4128 is shown at
the right.

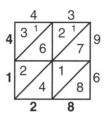

Legs of a Right Triangle (URG Unit 15; SG Unit 15)
The two sides of a right triangle that form the right angle.

Length of a Rectangle (URG Unit 4 & Unit 15;
SG Unit 4 & Unit 15)
The distance along one side of a rectangle.

Line
A set of points that form a straight path extending infi-
nitely in two directions.

Line of Reflection (URG Unit 10)
A line that acts as a mirror so that after a shape is flipped
over the line, corresponding points are at the same distance (equidistant) from the line.

Line Segment (URG Unit 14)
A part of a line between and including two points, called
the endpoints.

Liter (URG Unit 13)
Metric unit used to measure volume. A liter is a little
more than a quart.

Lowest Terms (SG Unit 11)
A fraction is in lowest terms if the numerator and
denominator have no common factor greater than 1.

M

Manipulated Variable (URG Unit 4; SG Unit 4)
In an experiment, the variable with values known at the
beginning of the experiment. The experimenter often
chooses these values before data is collected. The manipulated variable is often called the independent variable.

Mass (URG Unit 13)
The amount of matter in an object.

Mean (URG Unit 1 & Unit 4; SG Unit 1 & Unit 4)
An average of a set of numbers that is found by adding
the values of the data and dividing by the number of
values.

Measurement Division (URG Unit 4)
Division as equal grouping. The total number of objects
and the number of objects in each group are known. The
number of groups is the unknown. For example, tulip
bulbs come in packages of 8. If 216 bulbs are sold, how
many packages are sold?

Median (URG Unit 1; SG Unit 1)
For a set with an odd number of data arranged in order,
it is the middle number. For an even number of data
arranged in order, it is the mean of the two middle
numbers.

Meniscus (URG Unit 13)
The curved surface formed when a liquid creeps up the
side of a container (for example, a graduated cylinder).

Milliliter (ml) (URG Unit 13)
A measure of capacity in the metric system that is the
volume of a cube that is one centimeter long on each
side.

Mixed Number (URG Unit 3; SG Unit 3)
A number that is written as a whole number followed by
a fraction. It is equal to the sum of the whole number and
the fraction.

Mode (URG Unit 1; SG Unit 1)
The most common value in a data set.

Mr. Origin (URG Unit 10; SG Unit 10)
A plastic figure used to represent the origin of a coordinate system and to indicate the directions of the x- and
y- axes. (and possibly the z-axis).

N

N-gon (URG Unit 6; SG Unit 6)
A polygon with N sides.

Negative Number (URG Unit 10; SG Unit 10)
A number less than zero; a number to the left of zero on a
horizontal number line.

Nonagon (URG Unit 6; SG Unit 6)
A nine-sided polygon.

Numerator (URG Unit 3; SG Unit 3)
The number written above the line in a fraction. For
example, the 2 is the numerator in the fraction $\frac{2}{5}$. In this
case, we are interested in two of the five parts. (*See also*
denominator.)

Numerical Expression (URG Unit 4; SG Unit 4)
A combination of numbers and operations, e.g.,
$5 + 8 \div 4$.

Numerical Variable (URG Unit 1; SG Unit 1)
Variables with values that are numbers. (*See also* variable
and value.)

O

Obtuse Angle (URG Unit 6; SG Unit 6)
An angle that measures more than 90°.

Obtuse Triangle (URG Unit 6 & Unit 15; SG Unit 6 &
Unit 15)
A triangle that has an obtuse angle.

Octagon (URG Unit 6; SG Unit 6)
An eight-sided polygon.

Ordered Pair (URG Unit 10; SG Unit 10)
A pair of numbers that gives the coordinates of a point on
a grid in relation to the origin. The horizontal coordinate
is given first; the vertical coordinate is given second. For
example, the ordered pair (5, 3) gives the coordinates
of the point that is 5 units to the right of the origin and
3 units up.

Origin (URG Unit 10; SG Unit 10)
The point at which the *x*- and *y*-axes intersect on a
coordinate plane. The origin is described by the ordered
pair (0, 0) and serves as a reference point so that all the
points on the plane can be located by ordered pairs.

P

Pack (URG Unit 2; SG Unit 2)
A cube that measures 10 cm
on each edge. It is one of
the base-ten pieces and is
often used to represent 1000.
(*See also* base-ten pieces.)

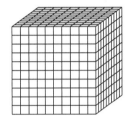

Parallel Lines
(URG Unit 6 & Unit 10)
Lines that are in the same direction. In the plane, parallel
lines are lines that do not intersect.

Parallelogram (URG Unit 6)
A quadrilateral with two pairs of parallel sides.

Partial Product (URG Unit 2)
One portion of the multiplication process in the all-partials multiplication method, e.g., in the problem 3 × 186
there are three partial products: 3 × 6 = 18,
3 × 80 = 240, and 3 × 100 = 300. (*See also*
all-partials multiplication method.)

Partitive Division (URG Unit 4)
Division as equal sharing. The total number of objects
and the number of groups are known. The number of
objects in each group is the unknown. For example,
Frank has 144 marbles that he divides equally into 6
groups. How many marbles are in each group?

Pentagon (URG Unit 6; SG Unit 6)
A five-sided polygon.

Percent (URG Unit 7; SG Unit 7)
Per hundred or out of 100. A special ratio that compares a
number to 100. For example, 20% (twenty percent) of the
jelly beans are yellow means that out of every 100 jelly
beans, 20 are yellow.

Perimeter (URG Unit 15; SG Unit 15)
The distance around a two-dimensional shape.

Period (SG Unit 2)
A group of three places in
a large number, starting on
the right, often separated by
commas as shown at the
right.

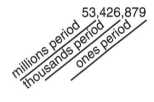

Perpendicular Lines (URG Unit 14 & Unit 15;
SG Unit 14)
Lines that meet at right angles.

Pi (π) (URG Unit 14; SG Unit 14)
The ratio of the circumference to diameter of a circle.
π = 3.14159265358979. . . . It is a nonterminating,
nonrepeating decimal.

Place (SG Unit 2)
The position of a digit in a number.

Place Value (URG Unit 2; SG Unit 2)
The value of a digit in a number. For example, the 5 is in
the hundreds place in 4573, so it stands for 500.

Polygon (URG Unit 6; SG Unit 6)
A two-dimensional connected figure made of line segments in which each endpoint of every side meets with
an endpoint of exactly one other side.

Population (URG Unit 1 Unit 1)
A collection of persons or things whose properties will
be analyzed in a survey or experiment.

Portfolio (URG Unit 2; SG Unit 2)
A collection of student work that show how a student's
skills, attitudes, and knowledge change over time.

Positive Number (URG Unit 10; SG Unit 10)
A number greater than zero; a number to the right of zero
on a horizontal number line.

Power (URG Unit 2; SG Unit 2)
An exponent. Read 10^4 as, "ten to the fourth power" or
"ten to the fourth." We say 10,000 or 10^4 is the fourth
power of ten.

Prime Factorization (URG Unit 11; SG Unit 11)
Writing a number as a product of primes. The prime
factorization of 100 is 2 × 2 × 5 × 5.

Prime Number (URG Unit 11; SG Unit 11)
A number that has exactly two factors: itself and 1.
For example, 7 has exactly two distinct factors, 1 and 7.

Probability (URG Unit 7; SG Unit 1 & Unit 7)
A number from 0 to 1 (0% to 100%) that describes how likely an event is to happen. The closer that the probability of an event is to one, the more likely the event will happen.

Product (URG Unit 2; SG Unit 2)
The answer to a multiplication problem. In the problem $3 \times 4 = 12$, 12 is the product.

Proper Fraction (URG Unit 3; SG Unit 3)
A fraction in which the numerator is less than the denominator. Proper fractions are less than one.

Proportion (URG Unit 3 & Unit 13; SG Unit 13)
A statement that two ratios are equal.

Protractor (URG Unit 6; SG Unit 6)
A tool for measuring angles.

Q

Quadrants (URG Unit 10; SG Unit 10)
The four sections of a coordinate grid that are separated by the axes.

Quadrilateral (URG Unit 6; SG Unit 6)
A polygon with four sides. (*See also* polygon.)

Quotient (URG Unit 4 & Unit 9; SG Unit 2, Unit 4, & Unit 9)
The answer to a division problem. In the problem $12 \div 3 = 4$, the 4 is the quotient.

R

Radius (URG Unit 14; SG Unit 14)
1. A line segment connecting the center of a circle to any point on the circle.
2. The length of this line segment.

Ratio (URG Unit 3 & Unit 12; SG Unit 3 & Unit 13)
A way to compare two numbers or quantities using division. It is often written as a fraction.

Ray (URG Unit 6; SG Unit 6)
A part of a line with one endpoint that extends indefinitely in one direction.

Rectangle (URG Unit 6; SG Unit 6)
A quadrilateral with four right angles.

Reflection (URG Unit 10)
(*See* flip.)

Regular Polygon (URG Unit 6; SG Unit 6; DAB Unit 6)
A polygon with all sides of equal length and all angles equal.

Remainder (URG Unit 4 & Unit 9; SG Unit 4 & Unit 9)
Something that remains or is left after a division problem. The portion of the dividend that is not evenly divisible by the divisor, e.g., $16 \div 5 = 3$ with 1 as a remainder.

Repeating Decimals (SG Unit 9)
A decimal fraction with one or more digits repeating without end.

Responding Variable (URG Unit 4; SG Unit 4)
The variable whose values result from the experiment. Experimenters find the values of the responding variable by doing the experiment. The responding variable is often called the dependent variable.

Rhombus (URG Unit 6; SG Unit 6)
A quadrilateral with four equal sides.

Right Angle (URG Unit 6; SG Unit 6)
An angle that measures 90°.

Right Triangle (URG Unit 6 & Unit 15; SG Unit 6 & Unit 15)
A triangle that contains a right angle.

Rubric (URG Unit 1)
A scoring guide that can be used to guide or assess student work.

S

Sample (URG Unit 1)
A part or subset of a population.

Scalene Triangle (URG Unit 15)
A triangle that has no sides that are equal in length.

Scientific Notation (URG Unit 2; SG Unit 2)
A way of writing numbers, particularly very large or very small numbers. A number in scientific notation has two factors. The first factor is a number greater than or equal to one and less than ten. The second factor is a power of 10 written with an exponent. For example, 93,000,000 written in scientific notation is 9.3×10^7.

Septagon (URG Unit 6; SG Unit 6)
A seven-sided polygon.

Side-Angle-Side (URG Unit 6 & Unit 14)
A geometric property stating that two triangles having two corresponding sides with the included angle equal are congruent.

Side-Side-Side (URG Unit 6)
A geometric property stating that two triangles having corresponding sides equal are congruent.

Sides of an Angle (URG Unit 6; SG Unit 6)
The sides of an angle are two rays with the same endpoint. (*See also* endpoint and ray.)

Sieve of Eratosthenes (SG Unit 11)
A method for separating prime numbers from nonprime numbers developed by Eratosthenes, an Egyptian librarian, in about 240 BCE.

Similar (URG Unit 6; SG Unit 6)
Similar shapes have the same shape but not necessarily the same size.

Skinny (URG Unit 2; SG Unit 2)
A block that measures 1 cm × 1 cm × 10 cm.
It is one of the base-ten pieces
and is often used to represent 10.
(*See also* base-ten pieces.)

Slide (URG Unit 10; SG Unit 10)
Moving a geometric figure in the plane by moving every point of the figure the same distance in the same direction. Also called translation.

Speed (URG Unit 3 & Unit 5; SG Unit 3 & Unit 5)
The ratio of distance moved to time taken, e.g.,
3 miles/1 hour or 3 mph is a speed.

Square (URG Unit 6 & Unit 14; SG Unit 6)
A quadrilateral with four equal sides and four right angles.

Square Centimeter (URG Unit 4; SG Unit 4)
The area of a square that is 1 cm long on each side.

Square Number (URG Unit 11)
A number that is the product of a whole number multiplied by itself. For example, 25 is a square number since $5 \times 5 = 25$. A square number can be represented by a square array with the same number of rows as columns. A square array for 25 has 5 rows of 5 objects in each row or 25 total objects.

Standard Form (SG Unit 2)
The traditional way to write a number, e.g., standard form for three hundred fifty-seven is 357. (*See also* expanded form and word form.)

Standard Units (URG Unit 4)
Internationally or nationally agreed-upon units used in measuring variables, e.g., centimeters and inches are standard units used to measure length and square centimeters and square inches are used to measure area.

Straight Angle (URG Unit 6; SG Unit 6)
An angle that measures 180°.

T

Ten Percent (URG Unit 4; SG Unit 4)
10 out of every hundred or $\frac{1}{10}$.

Tessellation (URG Unit 6 & Unit 10; SG Unit 6)
A pattern made up of one or more repeated shapes that completely covers a surface without any gaps or overlaps.

Translation
(*See* slide.)

Trapezoid (URG Unit 6)
A quadrilateral with exactly one pair of parallel sides.

Triangle (URG Unit 6; SG Unit 6)
A polygon with three sides.

Triangulating (URG Unit 6; SG Unit 6)
Partitioning a polygon into two or more nonoverlapping triangles by drawing diagonals that do not intersect.

Turn-Around Facts (URG Unit 2)
Multiplication facts that have the same factors but in a different order, e.g., $3 \times 4 = 12$ and $4 \times 3 = 12$. (*See also* commutative property of multiplication.)

Twin Primes (URG Unit 11; SG Unit 11)
A pair of prime numbers whose difference is 2. For example, 3 and 5 are twin primes.

U

Unit Ratio (URG Unit 13; SG Unit 13)
A ratio with a denominator of one.

V

Value (URG Unit 1; SG Unit 1)
The possible outcomes of a variable. For example, red, green, and blue are possible values for the variable *color*. Two meters and 1.65 meters are possible values for the variable *length*.

Variable (URG Unit 1; SG Unit 1)
1. An attribute or quantity that changes or varies. (*See also* categorical variable and numerical variable.)
2. A symbol that can stand for a variable.

Variables in Proportion (URG Unit 13; SG Unit 13)
When the ratio of two variables in an experiment is always the same, the variables are in proportion.

Velocity (URG Unit 5; SG Unit 5)
Speed in a given direction. Speed is the ratio of the distance traveled to time taken.

Vertex (URG Unit 6; SG Unit 6)
A common point of two rays or line segments that form an angle.

Volume (URG Unit 13)
The measure of the amount of space occupied by an object.

W

Whole Number
Any of the numbers 0, 1, 2, 3, 4, 5, 6 and so on.

Width of a Rectangle (URG Unit 4 & Unit 15; SG Unit 4 & Unit 15)
The distance along one side of a rectangle is the length and the distance along an adjacent side is the width.

Word Form (SG Unit 2)
A number expressed in words, e.g., the word form for 123 is "one hundred twenty-three." (*See also* expanded form and standard form.)

X

Y

Z